W9-BXY-728

ONLY YOU CAN BE YOU

ONLY YOU CAN BE YOU

21 *Days to Making Your Life Count*

ERIK REES

PASTOR OF LIFE MISSION, SADDLEBACK CHURCH

HOWARD BOOKS
A DIVISION OF SIMON & SCHUSTER
New York   London   Toronto   Sydney

Our purpose at Howard Books is to:
• *Increase faith* in the hearts of growing Christians
• *Inspire holiness* in the lives of believers
• *Instill hope* in the hearts of struggling people everywhere
Because He's coming again!

 Published by Howard Books, a division of Simon & Schuster, Inc.
1230 Avenue of the Americas, New York, NY 10020
www.howardpublishing.com

Only You Can Be You © 2009 Erik Rees

ISBN 978-1-4165-7302-9
ISBN 978-1-4391-6835-6 (ebook)

1   3   5   7   9   10   8   6   4   2

HOWARD and colophon are registered trademarks of Simon & Schuster, Inc.

Manufactured in the United States of America

For information regarding special discounts for bulk purchases, please contact: Simon & Schuster
Special Sales at 1-866-506-1949 or business@simonandschuster.com.

The Simon & Schuster Speakers Bureau can bring authors to your live event.
For more information or to book an event contact the Simon & Schuster Speakers Bureau at
866-248-3049 or visit our website at www.simonspeakers.com.

Cover design by Rick Brotherton
Edited by Between the Lines
Interior design by Davina Mock-Maniscalco

To my wife, Stacey,
thank you for showing me how to live with the courage
to be all God made me to be.
You model the message "only you can be you"
with confidence and grace.
Your impact on my life is influencing thousands worldwide.
I love you!

ACKNOWLEDGMENTS

I'M FOREVER GRATEFUL TO the following people who have shared in my dream for empowering people to become all God created them to be:

My Lord, I'm nothing without you! Thank you for personally teaching me the lesson that "only you can be you," for making me one of a kind, and for empowering me to make my life count for you.

Stacey, I'm so in love with you! I couldn't have done this one without you. I'm grateful for your encouragement, patience, and willingness to put aside your dreams for a while so I can follow one of mine.

To Shaya, Jessica, and J.T.—thanks for giving Daddy the freedom to write. You inspire me every day to live life with passion and joy. May you always have the inner confidence to be all God made you to be.

To Jeff—thanks for being my accountability partner. I'm a better man, husband, and father because of your constant cheers and challenges. Our weekly time together has not always been fun, but it has kept me focused on living my life for God.

To Peggy—I am so grateful for you. Your support, research, edits, and constant encouragement kept me writing when I felt like stopping. Thank you!

To Nancy—I'm blessed to have you as my agent. Your gifts of encouragement and discernment have been blessings in my life.

To Denny and the Howard team—thanks for your guidance and wisdom. May all our efforts bring glory to God!

FOREWORD

EVERY LIVING THING CREATED by God is made for a unique purpose—that includes you! Everything about you was thought about by God, designed by God, and programmed by God in order to make you exactly who you are. You are 100 percent original. That means you have something special to do that only you can do. In fact, if you don't do it, the world will miss out on what your contribution was meant to be. This stunning revelation, imbedded throughout Scripture, runs counter to much of today's popular teaching, which is rooted in the idea that life just "happened" and therefore has no ultimate meaning.

Nothing could be further from the truth! In fact, God says that you are so uniquely designed that *only you can be you.* That is the central message of this book by Erik Rees, and it's one I personally know that he has learned firsthand. Erik has served with me at Saddleback Church for over twelve years. When God reveals himself in your life as he has to Erik, you are never the same from that day forward. Erik has traveled the globe sharing this message in seminars and church services, and now he delivers it to you in an easy to grasp, twenty-one-day format. This book uncovers the layers God has built inside you, and when you discover them, you'll find true significance and freedom at long last—and isn't that what we're all looking for?

So grab a friend and enjoy discovering the powerful truth that only *you* can be you!

Rick Warren,
author of *The Purpose Driven Life*

CONTENTS

Acknowledgments   vii

Foreword   ix

Preface   Who Are You?   xiii

Introduction   Your Moment   1

Life Choice 1: *Surrender Your Life Completely*

Day 1   Restoration   21

Day 2   Surround Sound   33

Day 3   Cravings   43

Day 4   Scrapes and Scars   51

Day 5   Today   61

Day 6   Dreams and Desires   71

Day 7   Moving Day   79

Life Choice 2: *Steward Your Unique Style Wisely*

Day 8   Life on Loan   89

Day 9   Treasure Chest   97

Day 10   For You   107

Day 11   Jesus Calling   119

Day 12   Roller Coaster   129

Day 13   Seasonings   139

Day 14   Inside the Box   149

Life Choice 3: *Serve Others Passionately*

Day 15   Apron   161

Day 16   Hallways   171

Day 17   Takeout   181

Day 18   Does the Body Good   191

Day 19   Life Support   199

Day 20   Deposits   209

Day 21   Hourglass   219

Afterword: Living with Purpose

Day 22   Eye on the Prize   229

Appendix   What's in Your Box? (Assessing Your
               God-Given Tools)   239

Explanation of Spiritual Gifts   243

Small Group Discussion Questions   253

Notes   256

PREFACE
Who Are You?

As a kid, all I heard were negative messages about myself. "You'll never amount to anything!" my alcoholic dad told me over and over. In order to soften his blows—both the verbal and physical—I ate myself into oblivion. Somehow I made it to adulthood, but I was solidly on the wrong track. I arrived in corporate America totally focused on gaining success at any cost. Looking back, I was a perfect candidate for a heart attack by the age of thirty. How I kept from having one is a miracle I can credit only to God. All my life, I'd been trying to measure up to someone else's idea of who I should be. I had no idea who I really was.

So the first time I heard the words, "Only you can be you," it was as if a bucket of cold water had been splashed in my face. What? Could it be true?

Today I'm a pastor and life coach, and I've learned that not only is this message true but it's pivotal and life-changing. God has given me the privilege of seeing this message change the lives of thousands of people as I've shared it around the world, and I'm confident it will change your life, too. When you realize that only you can be you and that God has created you with a specific purpose in life, you'll be on your way to living the life you were born to live—a life of freedom and fulfillment.

So I invite you to accompany me on a journey for the next twenty-one days—a journey to a life that truly counts. When you grasp the concepts we're going to discuss, you'll see life through new eyes, and you'll wonder why you didn't see it before. That's how God is. When we ask him, he reveals to us the answers about our lives that can truly set us free. After all, it was God who created us to begin with.

We live in an age of great confusion regarding our identity. As if it were not enough to be pressured by others to be someone we are not or to act in ways to please them, the media are constantly sending strong messages about how we should look, what we should wear, whom we should date, where we should go, and various other life choices. The workplace makes us think we are expendable . . . replaceable . . . just a box on an organizational chart. Our culture, which is growing more secular by the day, wants us to believe we are here only by accident.

None of this is true. I know this because God's Word tells me so. And what God wants you to know is that *you are unique.* You are not an accident but an intentionally created being born into an intentional family at an intentional time for an intentional purpose. What's more, you are not replaceable. You are a Master-designed, handcrafted original. When you are gone, there will not be another you.

The truth is, you are who God made you to be—and *only you can be you.*

That's the central message of this book, and it's one I long for you to really get. When you do, it will set you free in ways you cannot imagine, just as it did for me when I first heard those words from my pastor, Rick Warren. For years I'd been playing the game, trying to be what my father wanted me to be or who society said I should be. When I finally realized that I was meant to be *me,* and that only *I* could do that job— well, it literally changed my life. And it will change yours, too.

In recent years it has been my privilege to travel the United States and much of the world delivering this life-changing message. It has become clear to me that many of you can identify with this message.

Why does this message matter? It matters because you were put here to do something special for God. And he has given you one lifetime, one moment, as it were, to accomplish that task. If you miss it, the world will go on . . . but you will have missed your reason for living. I don't believe you want to do that. The secret to fulfilling your mission is to realize that God created you on purpose—and then live intentionally for him.

YOUR MOMENT

Make a careful exploration of who you are and the work you
have been given, and then sink yourself into that.
Don't be impressed with yourself. Don't compare yourself with
others. Each of you must take responsibility for doing the creative
best you can with your own life.
Galatians 6:4–5 MSG

Just think, you're not here not by chance,
but by God's choosing. His hand formed you and made you the
person you are. He compares you to no one else—you are one of
a kind. You lack nothing that His grace can't give you. He has
allowed you to be here at this time in history to fulfill
His special purpose for this generation.
Roy Lessin

D ON'T WASTE YOUR LIFE.
"That little girl made a difference in my life," the man said as
he wiped tears from his eyes. He was filing out of a funeral service I'd
just conducted for an infant, the daughter of his friends. We shared only
a few words, but I'll never forget what else he said: "Make your life
count too."

Lea's life, from start to finish, had only been four months long.

Out in the parking lot, I climbed into my car to head home. I remember the sun's rays striking my cheek with intensity. I put the key in the ignition, but for some reason I didn't start the car. Those four short words echoed in my mind: "Make your life count." I must have repeated them thirty or forty times as I sat in my car reflecting on my life.

Was I making my life count? Who would say I'd made an impact on them? Was I living in such a way that the sum of my life really counted? Or was I just wasting my life? How could a four-month-old have made such an impact on others when her life was over before it had really even gotten started?

In the stillness of that moment, I asked God to forgive me for the times I hadn't lived solely for him. I pleaded earnestly for the strength and wisdom to make every moment from that day forward count for him. The Bible says, "A wise person thinks a lot about death, while a fool thinks only about having a good time" (Ecclesiastes 7:4 NLT).

I'm not someone who dwells on death, but I fully realize that I've got only one shot at making sure my life counts. And so do you.

One Life to Live

The truth of the matter is, you and I each have only one life to live, one "moment" on earth. That moment may last more than eighty years or, as with Lea, it may span only a few months. Whatever time God grants us on earth is our moment—and it's fleeting. The Bible says, "Teach us to number our days and recognize how few they are; help us spend them as we should" (Psalm 90:12 TLB).

From the beginning God has allowed us to decide how we will use the lives he has given us. Some people operate on cruise control, taking things as they come. Others consume their moment, striving to gain everything they can. They live by the motto, "He who dies with the most stuff wins." Still others make the most of their moment by contributing to the world around them. These are the people who focus on leaving the world better than they found it. Their motto is, "He who dies with the most changed lives wins."

Lea hadn't even developed the ability to talk, yet she could make all your worries disappear simply by looking into your eyes. I had experienced this phenomenon myself, two months earlier, at her baby dedication. Lea made a difference in my life, too. And I knew that when Lea entered the presence of her loving, heavenly Father, she heard him say, "Well done." Those are the same words I long to hear God say about my life. Don't you?

As I continued to reflect on my life as I sat in my car, I pulled out my journal and started to write about this experience. I thought about what would matter one hundred years from now, and I realized that not much of this material life would—not what type of car I drove, what size house I lived in, what title I had, how much money was in my bank account, or how I looked. But by deciding to make my life count for Christ, I could leave the world a better place than it was when I had entered it. On the drive home, I thanked God for using Lea's life to recalibrate mine.

What about you? Are you living a life that makes God the hero and you his helper? How is your life going to count?

We all leave a trail behind us on earth. It may evaporate quickly, like the trail of a shooting star, or we may leave a lasting heritage. What will your legacy look like? Will you allow God to use your one and only life to make a difference for him? Will you live your life intentionally, every day, for God? Will you redirect, focus, and maximize all he has given you for his glory? Will you follow Paul's example: "I consider my life worth nothing to me, if only I may finish the race and complete the task the Lord Jesus has given me—the task of testifying to the gospel of God's grace" (Acts 20:24)?

The apostle Paul knew the time was coming when God would review his life. He knew he had a lot in his past to make up for, and he longed to live out the rest of his days in such a way that God would be both pleased and glorified.

The Bible says this day will also come for you and me: "Each of us will give an account of himself to God" (Romans 14:12).

Why not let God recalibrate your life, too?

The Two Greatest Goals in Life

When I think about what really counts to God, I find myself overwhelmed by all the wonderful things God is teaching me.

Moses' legacy was to give us the top ten things God wanted people to focus on. That list wasn't just for then—God's Top Ten are still essential today. When Jesus came along, he simplified them and gave us two primary goals to achieve in life. Number one, he said, is to "Love the Lord your God with all your heart and with all your soul and with all your mind and with all your strength" (Mark 12:30). The second is to "Love your neighbor as yourself" (Mark 12:31). To emphasize his point, Jesus said, "There is no commandment greater than these" (Mark 12:31).

Some people may try to tell you it's not as simple as this, but Jesus says it is. Loving God and loving others is what life is all about. Jesus didn't say the goals of life were success and satisfaction. He didn't talk about making money or being popular. He didn't even mention making sure our title at work sounds important.

You may have heard it said, "You never see a hearse pulling a U-Haul trailer." It's true. As John Ortberg wrote, "When the game is over, it all goes back in the box."[1] Whatever we amassed here on earth stays here on earth. So if we're to make every day of our lives count for Christ, our goals must match his: to love God and to love others.

The Bible tells us that we must not only hear God's Word: we must put it into practice. James says, "Don't just listen to God's Word. You must do what it says. . . . If you do what it says and don't forget what you heard, then God will bless you for doing it" (James 1:22, 25 NLT). When we allow God's Word to direct our lives, we will accomplish what God wants us to do. We'll live a life that counts, and one day we'll hear God say, "Well done."

The Three Biggest Choices in Life

One Saturday I was helping my son, J.T., dig worms from the mud in our backyard. After a while I noticed that J.T. was carefully picking something out of the bucket. "What are you doing?" I asked.

"I'm taking the rocks out so they don't hurt the worms."

It got me thinking that our lives are like that bucket. And to keep the rocks from hurting us or hindering us from achieving the two greatest goals in life, we need to make three key choices.

I'm not talking about the choices we make every day: when to get up, what to wear, what to eat, where to go, what to do, whom to call, and what emails to answer. While these daily decisions have some importance, they don't do much to influence the two life goals Jesus gave us.

However, we can make several key decisions every day that do impact every facet of our lives. Here are what I believe to be the three greatest choices we can make in life:

1. Surrender your life completely.
2. Steward your unique style wisely.
3. Serve others passionately.

We'll spend a lot of time in the days ahead diving deeper into each of these choices, but here they are in a nutshell.

Life Choice 1: Surrender Your Life Completely

I urge you, brothers, in view of God's mercy,
to offer your bodies as living sacrifices,
holy and pleasing to God—
this is your spiritual act of worship.

—Romans 12:1

Offering your body translates into surrendering everything in your life—your heart, your mind, your strength, your soul, your dreams, your desires, your insecurities, your past, your present, your relationships, your finances, your jobs, your kids, your pride, and your potential. It includes asking God to help you sort out the rocks as well. What has come into your life along the way that's hindering you from reaching your goals?

God made you and planned every day of your life before you were ever born. You owe it to him to offer back for his use what he has given you. Surrendering your life means giving God full control. Have you heard the Carrie Underwood song "Jesus, Take the Wheel"? It tells the story of a young woman whose life is out of control and whose car is about to crash. Desperate, she calls out to the Lord. That's the mental picture I get when I think of surrendering my life. Surrendering to God is about recognizing that without him, my life is out of control. When I surrender, I yield to him full control over my choices.

The Bible says, "Give yourselves completely to God, for you were dead, but now you have new life. So use your whole body as an instrument to do what is right for the glory of God" (Romans 6:13 NLT). That word, *completely,* can be pretty intimidating. Many years ago I asked God to be the boss of my life. I let him run the show, but only when I needed him. I wasn't ready to give myself to God completely. As a young man on my way up the corporate ladder, I enjoyed chasing cash. I wanted the biggest office, the most prestigious title, and a major bank account. I wanted to control my career and my relationships. I wanted God, but I wasn't willing to *completely* surrender my life. I liked my comfort.

In time I discovered that comfort does not produce growth. The fact is, God is far more focused on my growth and character development than on my comfort. Jesus said, "If you love me, obey my commandments" (John 14:15 NLT). He wants us to let go of the meaningless things we think define us and follow him completely.

I'm reminded of a group of guys Jesus asked to follow him. Because they loved Jesus, they didn't think twice about following him. They didn't waste time worrying about their careers, their incomes, or their identities. Instead, they made the most significant choice they could with their lives—to surrender everything and obey.

That same choice is set before us today. God loves us too much to make us his puppets. He gave us free will. That means we can choose whether we'll obey him. It's our nature to want to be in control, but when we surrender that control to him, we will discover to our delight that God helps us. As Philippians 2:13 says, "God is working in you, giving you the desire and the power to do what pleases him" (NLT).

Control is the opposite of surrender. When we're in control, we've selected to move God out of the center of our lives. And then we wonder why we worry more, experience more stress, have no peace, and end up wandering through life. The Bible tells us that yielding control to God brings us peace and other great rewards: "Surrender to God All-Powerful! You will find peace and prosperity. Listen to his teachings and take them to heart" (Job 22:21–22 CEV).

The Bible also promises us real rest: "Are you tired? Worn out? Burned out on religion? Come to me. Get away with me and you'll recover your life. I'll show you how to take a real rest. Walk with me and work with me—watch how I do it. Learn the unforced rhythms of grace" (Matthew 11:28–29 MSG).

This first choice we must make is to connect with God and live our lives 100 percent for him. Having a connection with God is what Jesus said was the key to a life of significance: "I am the vine; you are the branches. If a man remains in me and I in him, he will bear much fruit; apart from me you can do nothing" (John 15:5). I don't want my life to accomplish nothing—I want it to count for Christ! And I believe you do, too.

Surrendering to God completely helps answer the question, Whom will I live for, God or myself? This may sound like a paradox, but the benefit gained from surrendering is freedom. When we surrender, we become free from our past, free to live each day for God, and free to fulfill our true purpose in life. The surrendered heart is free of regrets, worries, wrongs, and wounds. True freedom is found only in relationship with Jesus: "If the Son sets you free, you will be free indeed" (John 8:36). If you long for lasting freedom in your life, then choose to surrender completely to God.

The bottom line is this: only you can be you, and only you can choose to surrender your life completely to God, rocks and all.

Will you?

Life Choice 2: Steward Your Unique Style Wisely

From everyone who has been given much,
much will be demanded; and from the one
who has been entrusted with much,
much more will be asked.
—Luke 12:48

Stewardship means "the careful and responsible management of something entrusted to one's care."[2] You and I have been entrusted with a lot. God has given us our talents, our time, our passions, our money, our experiences, our relationships, and our vocations to manage and maximize for his glory.

Actor Denzel Washington recognizes that his abilities were given to him to use on behalf of others. One way in which Denzel stewards what he has been given is by acting as a national spokesman for the Boys & Girls Clubs of America, an organization of which he was formerly a member.[3]

Like Denzel, you and I have a responsibility to use what we have to bless others. I don't know what God has given you, but I know he made you special for a purpose. He has given you talents to help you make your life count. As the Bible tells us, we must be sure to use whatever gifts God has given us. "We have different gifts, according to the grace given us. If a man's gift is prophesying, let him use it in proportion to his faith. If it is serving, let him serve; if it is teaching, let him teach; if it is encouraging, let him encourage; if it is contributing to the needs of others, let him give generously; if it is leadership, let him govern diligently; if it is showing mercy, let him do it cheerfully" (Romans 12:6–8).

We must be careful to invest these gifts in ways that will yield the greatest returns—as determined by God's measuring stick. (That's not easy when the world is shouting at us that we own everything we have and that it's ours to do with as we please.) God says our gifts have value whether we are reaching five hundred people or only one person. The point is that we invest them for God and not for a short-term return.

Stewardship is not ownership. An owner takes control and often focuses on blessing himself first. An owner looks to gain more for himself, while a steward aims to gain more for his master—more money, more time, a higher return on the investment. It's vital that we remember we're stewards, not owners—not even in our own lives. We really don't own anything—it's all on loan from God while we're here on earth. We have nothing that hasn't been given to us by our Master. As stewards, it's our responsibility to use what God has given us to glorify him and to bless others.

What unique things has God loaned to you? What are your talents? What passions has God entrusted to you? What experiences have you had that can bless others?

In his book *The Purpose Driven Life,* Rick Warren wrote:

Only you can be you.

God designed each of us so there would be no duplication in the world. No one has the exact same mix of factors that make you unique. That means no one else on earth will ever be able to play the role God planned for you. If you don't make your unique contribution to the Body of Christ, it won't be made.[4]

Do you truly believe that only you can be you? It's true. Only you can live your life. Only you can steward the wonderful skills God has given you.

The problem is, most people have believed in a big lie. How often have you heard, "You can be anything you want to be"? That simply isn't true. Think about it—if you could be *anything* you wanted to be, you'd have the power to call up any talent you desired, and *poof! American Idol,* here I come. How many of us have wasted years wishing we could be something we simply were not made to be? People are not random, interchangeable collections of chromosomes with no master design behind them. God planned each one of us before we were even born.

That's great news! That means we don't have to try to be someone we aren't. All we have to be is who God made us to be.

One of my favorite passages is Psalm 139:13–16. It says, "You [God] made all the delicate, inner parts of my body and knit me together in my mother's womb. Thank you for making me so wonderfully complex! Your workmanship is marvelous—how well I know it. You watched me as I was being formed in utter seclusion, as I was woven together in the dark of the womb. You saw me before I was born. Every day of my life was recorded in your book. Every moment was laid out before a single day had passed" (NLT).

God has a great plan for our lives: " 'I know the plans I have for you,' declares the LORD, 'plans to prosper you and not to harm you, plans to give you hope and a future' " (Jeremiah 29:11). Why would we not want those plans? Choosing to pursue God's plan for our lives helps answer the question, What will I do with my life—will I consume it, cruise through it, or contribute in such a way that my life counts?

The benefit of wise stewardship is fruitfulness. When we try to do things we aren't good at, the result is frustration, lack of fulfillment, and stress. But when we do what we are designed to do, we excel and others are blessed. It only makes sense to use your life graciously for God.

Life Choice 3: Serve Others Passionately

Even the Son of Man
did not come to be served, but to serve,
and to give His life a ransom for many.
—Mark 10:45 NASB

Once we surrender our lives to God and begin living as stewards rather than owners, this last choice becomes really easy.

When we share our resources with others in need, we're serving God by serving people. The Bible says, "Never be lacking in zeal, but keep your spiritual fervor, serving the Lord. . . . Share with God's people who are in need. Practice hospitality" (Romans 12:11, 13). And Jesus said, "If you give even a cup of cold water to one of the least of my followers, you will surely be rewarded" (Matthew 10:42 NLT).

Not only is blessing others a great way to live our lives, but, as an added bonus, it always blesses us in return—often even more than it blesses the person we sought to serve. Serving is less about what you do than whom you do it for.

Choosing to serve others passionately means putting others' needs in front of my own, loving them, and giving as Jesus would. Serving God by serving others gives me lasting fulfillment, knowing that I'm following Jesus' example. Will others see the heart of a servant through your life?

Paul wrote, "I pray that your love will keep on growing and that you will fully know and understand how to make the right choices. Then you will still be pure and innocent when Christ returns. And until that day, Jesus Christ will keep you busy doing good deeds that bring glory and praise to God" (Philippians 1:9–11 CEV). That's my prayer for you, too. May this message stir up in you a strong desire to live your life for God, serving others and making every day count for all eternity.

As you reflect on the three Life Choices, let me ask you a question: Could you benefit from making a U-turn in your life? The You-Turn diagram, a method I came up with during my coaching sessions, is a great visual to quickly help a person determine where they are and where they want to go. Place an X near the words that represent your life today and a G next to the words indicating your goals for the future.

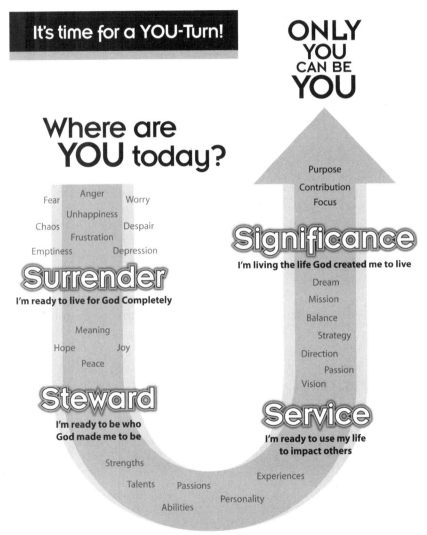

21 Days Together

Let's go back to J.T.'s bucket for a moment. When my son told me, "I'm taking out the rocks so they won't hurt the worms," I realized in that moment that each of our lives is like a bucket. We start out with what God has put in our buckets, but as we go through life, some rocks get thrown in. Will we make Life Choice 1 and surrender to God those rocks that weigh us down? Will we make Life Choice 2 and choose to use effectively what God has put in our bucket to honor him and help others? Finally, will we make Life Choice 3 to bless others by sharing with them what's in our bucket? These choices are what we'll be discussing over the next three weeks.

When I conduct life-coaching sessions, I typically choose a neighborhood coffee shop as the meeting place. I love the aroma of freshly brewed coffee that permeates the place and the casual setting that always says, "Come on in! Stay awhile." So, for the next twenty-one days, I invite you to imagine that we're hanging out at the local coffee shop each day for a chat. If coffee isn't your thing, I hear they have some killer noncoffee drinks, too. We'll sit at a table or sink into one of the comfortable booths and just talk about what it means to be the unique, God-designed you.

I decided on twenty-one days because someone once told me it takes that many days to form a habit. The habit I hope you develop is that of spending a little time each day with God so he can help you to make your life count for him. This habit can truly revolutionize your life. It has mine. Plugging in to the greatest power source in the world on a regular basis can turn an ordinary day into an extraordinary one. When we spend time with God, he can calm our stressful lives, clear our cluttered minds, and restore our tired souls. These are just a few of things I've personally experienced when I spend daily time with God.

Our goal over the next twenty-one days is to explore God's plan for making you and to help you discover what he has in mind for you. To that end, we'll share about thirty minutes or so together and then reflect on or respond to what we've shared. It's my hope that by the end of our journey, you'll be ready to craft a master plan for the life only you can live—a life that counts for God. A life that is hallmarked by surrender, stewardship, and service.

I would also encourage you to bring a friend with you to our time together. I've always learned the most when I discuss what I'm reading with others, whether it's my wife, my best friend, my mentor, or a few coworkers. Having the chance to bounce ideas off these key people has helped me press toward the goal of making my life count for Christ.

Whom could you invite to join us? Give them a call or send them an email. Better yet, buy them their own copies of *Only You Can Be You* and ask them to join you.

Do you love challenges? I hope so, because I have one for you. I challenge you to complete your daily reading and reflection questions each day for the next twenty-one days. No falling behind and no skipping ahead. Just read ten or so pages a day and complete the exercises. This challenge will take about twenty minutes a day. Will you accept the challenge? If so, register online today for *Only You Can Be You* 21 Day Connection. When you do, I will be able to send you daily coaching tips and you will be able to send me your goals, thoughts, and prayers along the way. I can't wait to hear your story.

Setting a Goal

Goals help keep us going when days get tough, and even though our trip is a relatively short one, I imagine we'll hit a pothole or two along the way.

When it comes to making their lives count, I've discovered that many people share similar emotions and motivations. While on a crazy conference tour in 2007, I had the privilege of leading several Only You Can Be You conferences in many states and countries. Everywhere I went, I found people who weren't living the life God had created them to live. From Brazil to Rwanda, England to India, Atlanta to Portland, and Santa Barbara to Orlando, God allowed me to encourage thousands of people, and I was blessed to watch him use this message to change their lives. I'm confident that it will change your life, too.

Many of the people I spoke with during those conferences seemed frantic, defeated, confused, exhausted, frustrated, overwhelmed, burned out, discouraged, or, sad to say, even suicidal.

Gordon had reached the end of his rope. In his view, his life had become a disaster. Just when he'd gotten himself on track and things were looking good, his wife left him. Only later did he learn that she had cheated on him for more than a year. He grieved for his young daughter, now living in a home with a man who was not her real dad. As we talked and prayed together, God revealed to Gordon that the pain in his life was not his fault. He saw that God created each of us with free will and that all too often we make selfish choices that hurt others. He understood that God has made each person unique, with his or her own story to be written. By the time we parted, Gordon realized it was up to him to choose God's way for his life and to trust God for his daughter's life, too.

I met many others who were frustrated with their jobs; unfulfilled; holding on to pain from their past; trying to please parents no longer living; longing for hope and peace. They all desired to find their purpose in life. They wanted to know who God had made them to be.

At the start of each conference, I asked people to answer two questions on a 3 x 5 inch card: On one side, what is your goal for being here? On the other side, how do you feel about your life?

Here are the typical responses I received from people all around the world:

What is your goal for being here?

- To find direction

- To gain hope

- To find freedom
- To gain clarity
- To find peace

- To restore my spirit

How do you feel about your life?

- I feel like I'm going really fast in the wrong direction.
- I feel like I'm in a dark valley and have no way out.
- I feel like my past is controlling me.
- I feel like life is passing me by.
- I feel like I'm constantly living for the next thing to do.
- I feel overloaded with too many things. I'm tired.

- To gain confidence
- To embrace my gifts

- To discover my calling
- To find my purpose for life
- To get back on track
- To discover my passions
- To find lasting fulfillment

- To develop a plan for my life

- I feel like I'm scared to succeed for God.
- I feel like I'm not using my strengths at all.
- I feel like my career is wearing me down.
- I feel overwhelmed by life.
- I feel stuck in a rut.
- I feel unmotivated in life.
- I long for a sense of lasting inner satisfaction.
- I feel lost, like I'm just wandering through life.

What about you? How would you answer those two questions? Please take the time to write out your answers to these two questions right now. Your answer to the first will become your goal for our time together. If you identify it, we can celebrate together with God when we reach it.

What is your goal for reading this book?

How do you feel about your life?

The most affirming part of flying those eighty-five thousand miles around the globe on a plane was reading the evaluations from my cozy coach window seat. As I did this, God allowed me to see that my life was making a difference for him. But those conferences were not about me—they were all about God.

Life is about loving God and others. It's my hope that by the time we're done, you will write a praise to God for helping you get closer to him. Here are a few praises from those evaluations:

- I'm finally free to be me!
- My life is going to count for Christ.
- I surrendered my life today.
- God is my rock.
- God has gifted me for greatness.
- God does have a plan for my life.
- I discovered my purpose today.
- My spirit is restored.
- I finally gave everything to him.
- I'm going to leave a legacy for him.
- God is going to be the hero of everything I do.
- I finally gave myself permission to be who he made me to be.
- It's okay to be a world-class mom.
- I don't have to please people anymore . . . just God.
- I can use my passions to serve people.

What if I told you that instead of feeling miserable, frustrated, and overwhelmed by life, you could be free, confident, joyful, loving, stable, and content? Do those words describe the kind of person you want to become? I have no idea how God is going to use the next twenty-one days to transform your life, but if you allow him to, he will do it.

This is not a self-help book. Rather, this is a spirit-help book. We can't make our lives count for Christ unless his Spirit is guiding us. In John 10:10 Jesus told us why he came to earth: I came so that everyone would have life, and have it in its fullest.

A full life is a life that counts for Christ.

At the end of our journey, I would love to hear what God has revealed to you. Just email me directly at erik@erikrees.com.

If you need to spend more time with someone to further clarify your life or craft your master life plan, I can connect you with someone who can help you—a certified life coach or a pastor—or I can help you find a small-group connection in your area. If you discover that part of your life design includes helping others reach their potential, let me know that, too. Being used by God to help another person make his or her life count for Christ is one of the most fulfilling experiences I've ever had. You may want to enroll in one of my certification courses. I want that kind of fulfillment for you, too.

During the months it took me to write this book, I thanked God every day for allowing me the honor of helping you. Although we may never personally meet, I want to thank you for allowing me to share my life with you over the next few weeks. As you will quickly learn, I'm not perfect, nor do I claim to be. But I do fully believe that God is perfect and that he will help me make my life count for Christ. He will do that for you, too, if you simply let him.

Ask him to show you what's in your bucket.

A Prayer for Our Time Together

Holy Father, please show us just how special you have made us. Use the next twenty-one days to take us wherever you need to so that we can experience you as we never have before. Ignite our hearts, God. Let them always burn for the things you desire most. Align our dreams and desires with yours.

Lord, use your Spirit to help us surrender our lives totally to you so that we can see just how wonderfully you have made us. Help us to be good stewards of all the wonderful, unique things you have given to us for your glory. Give us the strength to love people as you do and serve others as your Son did. Grant us continued grace, love, and wisdom as we walk this journey with you.

God, give us strength to face our fears along the way. Fill us with your love. Grant us faith as never before. Help us to move away from our comfort zones and closer to your calling.

Father, do whatever it takes to give us the clarity and the confidence to make our lives count for Christ. In Jesus' name, Amen.

See you tomorrow. May the coffee be warm enough to make you comfortable . . . and strong enough to get your attention.

LIFE CHOICE 1

Surrender Your Life Completely

Day 1

RESTORATION

Discovering the True You

The more we get what we now call "ourselves"
out of the way and let Him take us over,
the more truly ourselves we become.
—C.S. Lewis

The absolute surrender of everything into His hands
is necessary. If our hearts are willing for that, there is no limit
to what God will do for us or to the blessing He will bestow.
—Andrew Murray

W<small>E LOVED OUR HOME,</small> but after living there awhile, it seemed that something was wrong. That fireplace: it just didn't quite say, "Sit by me and get cozy." After a few years of watching the paint flake off, my wife, Stacey, said, "What would happen if we restored the bricks to their original color?" *Ugh,* I thought, picturing all the work it would take. *What would happen? Major headaches, that's what!*

"Sure, honey," I said. "Let's do it." And so the restoration process began. After the first few "guaranteed" products failed, we sought and followed a professional's advice (always a good idea). We took off the old paint, wire brushed the bricks, applied stain, and lost our tempers a few more times than I'm pleased to admit.

Then one day it was done. We stood back and admired the earthy red beauty of those bricks, looking just as their maker had intended. "It's beautiful!" our daughter Jessica exclaimed. "It was hard work, but it was worth it!" My aching muscles agreed. There's nothing quite like natural beauty.

We serve a God of restoration who wants to bring us back to his original design. While the fireplace had no choice about submitting to our renovation, you and I are free to choose whether we'll surrender to his control. On the surface, that sounds like an easy choice to make, like trusting the hairstylist to know what will look best on you. But in practice . . . well, let's just say that if it were easy, a lot of pastors would have nothing to do.

In the book of Deuteronomy, Moses impressed upon the children of Israel the importance of always choosing God's way over their own when he told them: "When you and your children return to the Lord your God and obey him with all your heart and with all your soul according to everything I command you today, then the Lord your God will restore your fortunes and have compassion on you and gather you again from all the nations where he scattered you" (Deuteronomy 30:2–3). God is ready and waiting to bring out his best in each one of us—but first we must surrender to him.

What Surrender Means

Many people have the wrong idea about what it means to surrender to God. In her book *Dangerous Surrender,* Kay Warren explains:

> *Surrender* is a dirty word to many of us. It has mostly negative connotations. Some synonyms are *give in, give up, admit defeat, lay down your arms, submit, yield, capitulate.* . . . One of the most deeply held illusions of Westerners such as me is that we are tough and independent and quite sure that we don't need anyone else. We carry these illusions over into our spiritual

lives as well, and doing so keeps many from following Christ. "Surrender to God? No thanks. I can do life by myself." Even those of us who have acknowledged our need for Jesus Christ to be our Savior have a difficult time surrendering our will to him on a daily basis; we're just too full of ourselves, too much in control, too proud."[1]

What Kay describes is exactly where I was when I first asked Christ into my life. I'd heard that I had a heavenly Father who loved me and wanted to help me. Believe me, I was ready for that message. After years of trying to please a dad who didn't really care and then trying to live up to a false image of myself, I was lonely and tired. But it was much later when I finally invited Jesus to be in the center of my life, where he belongs. When I finally switched places with God and fully surrendered to him, everything in my life changed. It was as if God had pushed the Reset button and restored the original settings that had been lost for all those years.

Today I'm living the life God intended for me from the beginning. He's taken all the junk I went through as a kid—the abusive, alcoholic father, my overeating to compensate for not feeling loved, the pressure I felt to live up to someone else's idea of perfection—and given me back the real Erik Rees. He has convinced me that only I can be me. And by the same token, only you can be you.

Anything You Want to Be— Or Who God Made You to Be?

I recently finished reading a great book, *Pinocchio Parenting: 21 Lies We Tell Our Kids,* by Chuck Borsellino. Guess what one of the top lies is that parents tell their kids? "You can be anything you want to be." Have you heard that phrase before? I have. Did you hear it growing up? I did. If you have kids now, have you ever told them that? I sure have. The phrase *you can be anything you want to be* sounds so good, doesn't it? But this idea has a big problem: it's a lie!

The truth is, you can't be anything you want to be. When you were born, you were given a specific set of gifts, talents, and passions, and a unique personality. Then, as you grew, you went through a series of experiences—some good and some not so good. Perhaps you even had a few devastating moments. All those things are tools God uses to make you into the unique you he's had in mind from the start. But you've got to let go and let the master makeover artist do his work.

Over the next few days, we'll look at various areas of our lives that we need to inventory to make sure we're living truly surrendered lives. We must give every aspect of our lives—our past, our present, and our future—to God so that he can guide us. In the weeks ahead, I'll ask you a few tough questions because I care about you and want to see you living the life that God intends for you—a life that many want but few take the time to strive toward. Although I truly desire to see you find freedom in who you are and what you do, what matters most is that God wants this for you. He designed you to be you and wants you to trust him with your life.

As you think about making this fresh start and renewed relationship, I must ask you a critical question—one of the most important you'll ever have to answer: where is God in your life right now? There are only three real possibilities. He is either:

1. Outside your life
2. Inside your life, or
3. At the center of your life

When God is outside our lives, he has no chance to finish his good work. When God is inside our lives, he'll control only what we give to him. However, when God is at the center, given full access, he can begin his work of restoring our broken lives.

So I ask you again, where is God in your life?

The Bible says, "GOD made my life complete when I placed all the pieces before him. When I got my act together, he gave me a fresh start. Now I'm alert to GOD's ways; I don't take God for granted. Every day I review the ways he works; I try not to miss a trick. I feel put back together, and I'm watching my step. GOD rewrote the text of my life when I opened the book of my heart to his eyes" (Psalm 18:20 MSG).

Could you use a fresh start with God? Do you feel like your life is an unfinished puzzle? God wants to put it back together—and only he knows where all the pieces go. He wants to rewrite the story of your life, but you've got to recognize that he has always been its author. The psalmist David knew what that felt like when he wrote, "Count yourself lucky, how happy you must be—you get a fresh start, your slate's wiped clean" (Psalm 32:1 MSG). If you want your slate wiped clean, you've got to give God the eraser. Are you catching the drift here? Give it all to God . . . that's what you do when you surrender.

The Surrendered Life = The Significant Life

We hear a lot of talk about living a significant life, as if it's something on the other side of the fence that we must work toward, the ultimate goal. But I would argue that we can live a significant life every day—once we understand God's equation: the surrendered life = the significant life.

Let's take a look at what God promises to those who choose the surrendered life, as opposed to continuing in a self-centered life. Following are the wonderful benefits of allowing God to live at the center of our lives.

Purpose for Living

As God prepared Moses to confront Pharaoh and demand that he release the Israelites from their Egyptian captivity, he said, "I have raised you up for this very purpose, that I might show you my power and that my name might be proclaimed in all the earth" (Exodus 9:16). You and I may not be called to lead a nation, but we all have the purpose of showing God's power through our lives so that his name will be glorified through us.

Paul tells us, "We are God's workmanship, created in Christ Jesus to do good works, which God prepared in advance for us to do" (Ephesians 2:10). Beyond showing God's power to the world through our lives, discovering our purpose allows us to see what God created us to do.

But discovering God's purpose for our lives is impossible unless we first surrender to him our dreams, our hopes, our plans, and our ambitions. The Bible says, "Many are the plans in a man's heart, but it is the LORD's purpose that prevails" (Proverbs 19:21).

God desires to show you the specific purpose he put you on earth to fulfill. That's great news!

Peace of Mind

Almost since time began, mankind has been on a quest for peace. Our world is continually in conflict, yet, somewhere in our hearts, we know this is not how it should be. We talk about peace, we put VISUALIZE WORLD PEACE bumper stickers on our cars, and at Christmastime we sing songs about peace on earth. So why is peace so elusive?

Jesus promised his disciples, "Peace I leave with you; my peace I give you. I do not give to you as the world gives. Do not let your hearts be troubled and do not be afraid" (John 14:27). This world may never have peace, but you can know the peace of God in your life. Surrender to him your troubled heart, your confusion, and your conflicts, and watch his peace take over.

Is peace of mind something you long for? If so, keep reading!

Perspective for Living

Have you ever noticed that people tend to line up on one side of an issue or the other? Jesus sees all sides—better yet, he knows what is true and what is false. In Christ we can finally know genuine right thinking. He helps us to see life as it really is.

We must be willing to see life through Jesus' eyes. In order to do that, we must be willing to surrender our old ideas and consider his radical call to righteous living. The Bible says, "Let God transform you into a new person by changing the way you think. Then you will learn to know God's will for you, which is good and pleasing and perfect" (Romans 12:2 NLT).

One of the coolest benefits of giving God the center place in our lives is his daily guidance. When God is truly the pilot of our lives, he grants us guidance for living. This guidance comes in the form of perspective. Situations in life that never made sense, we now begin to understand.

Power to Persevere

In my profession, I work with many people who want a quick fix. They want to meet with me once and be done. They want the confusion and chaos in their lives to be replaced with clarity and confidence, but they don't want to take the time this requires. This is another reason why we are spending twenty-one days together. I don't want you to give up. More important, I have discovered in my walk with God that he does not want me to ever give up. Tap into his power and persevere through the times of stress, pain, and difficulty. God does not promise us a pain-free life, but he does promise us the power to finish life faithful and fulfilled.

Plan to Live Out

None of us has a crystal ball, but if we did, we might be sorry to see some of the trouble coming our way. But no matter what tomorrow holds, we can be confident in God. " 'I know the plans I have for you,' declares the LORD, 'plans to prosper you and not to harm you, plans to give you hope and a future' " (Jeremiah 29:11). This does not absolve us from responsibility for making our own plans, but it does allow us to surrender the outcome of those plans to God, trusting that whatever happens, we are safe in his hands.

Symptoms of a Self-Centered Life

In contrast to the surrendered life, the self-centered life is a diseased one marked by several symptoms. I discovered three common symptoms during a ten-year study I did, looking at what caused people to seek change in their lives. More to the point, these were the factors that caused people who had kept God outside their lives to place him at the center.

As we look at these three symptoms, you may find that a few or all of them resonate with you. That's great! It means you truly desire to become all that God made you to be so that you can do all that God has planned for you.

Frustration of Mind

The first symptom of a self-centered life is a high level of frustration: frustration with careers, relationships, finances, marriage, kids . . . the list goes on. Frustration is really a symptom of an issue that goes deeper than the things that seem to frustrate us. It all goes back to the basic issue of control, to the self-centered wanting to be in charge of certain aspects of our lives instead of letting God be in control.

The truth is, without Christ we will remain frustrated and try to control every area of our lives. But when we surrender everything to God, our minds will be renewed and we'll get to see God's will for our lives. This is exactly what Paul taught in Romans 12:1–2, when he wrote, "I plead with you to give your bodies to God because of all he has done for you. Let them be a living and holy sacrifice—the kind he will find acceptable. This is truly the way to worship him. Don't copy the behavior and customs of this world, but let God transform you into a new person by changing the way you think. Then you will learn to know God's will for you, which is good and pleasing and perfect" (NLT).

We won't be frustrated with our lives when God gives us the opportunity to know our purpose and to know his desires for our lives.

Surrendering our entire lives to God allows his peace and purpose to calm our frustrations.

Fatigue of Heart

When a person keeps God outside his or her life or away from the center of life over long periods of time, frustration of mind turns into fatigue of heart. I've coached some of the most tired, sad, depressed people. These are great people whom Jesus died for but who still insist on remaining CEO of their own lives. When we hold on to control rather than surrender it to the One who made and sustains our lives, we become weary of trying so hard to get it right only to fail time after time.

Is your heart weary from the frustration of trying to steer your own life? Do you ever feel like you just can't take any more? Everyone has those "end of the rope" moments occasionally, but when you have given God ultimate control, you can rest in him until the storm blows over.

Fear of Life

When we continue to push God out of his rightful place at the center of our lives, fear sets in. We fear that we've messed up beyond remedy . . . that we're broken, inferior, unlovable, rejected. People in the grip of such fears have said to me, "Erik, I don't think I have a purpose in life." The saddest phrase I heard was from a young woman: "Erik, I don't think God loves me." Although that was just a lie from Satan, she believed it 100 percent. It was not until some months later that she replaced her fear with faith in God.

The self-centered life is afraid of death, afraid of losing everything, and thus focuses on survival. In so doing, such people fail to really live. While the drive to survive is universal and God given, we're in trouble when we have such fear of losing it that we hold on to life with a fierce grip, denying and fighting against the day that death will come. The person with a surrendered life realizes that we are here for only a moment—but that something better is coming. Pastor Rick Warren often quotes the old saying, "Only one life too soon is passed; only what's done for Christ will last." The fearful, self-centered person clings to this life, which he or she cannot keep. The surrendered person rests in God's promise of eternal life.

Malise provides an example of the change that can take place when a person living a self-centered life exchanges her frustration of mind, fatigue of heart, and fear of life for the purposes of living, peace of mind, perspective on life, power to persevere, and plans for life that come when we surrender our lives to God. After a lifetime of mental illness, Malise had finally reached bottom. "I was as low as I could possibly get," she told me. "I hadn't worked in months; I was repeatedly in the hospital due to harming myself. I was broken in every sense of the word. Frustration was at an all-time high.

"That's when God came to me. I can't explain just how, but it's like I heard a voice saying, 'You're going to be okay.' And immediately, my life began to change." Malise put God in the center of her life, and since then her life has steadily improved.

"By surrendering all I could possibly be—all my fears, loves, hopes, and dreams—to God and asking him to take care of me, I am now freer than I ever imagined I could be," she said. "I've learned that in everything I do, the point is to help others see that they can be free—free from whatever is holding them back."

Making It Count

How about you? Has our conversation today motivated you to surrender all to Christ? Does the word *surrender* still make you think of fear, weakness, or giving up? How has considering God's promises changed the way you think of surrender? Write your thoughts in the space below and share them with God, who loves you and wants you to feel safe in his presence. But first, let's pray.

Father, I confess that I've been living a self-centered life for way too long, and I'm so tired! As I work through this book, help me to understand the life you created me to live. For now, give me the strength to see that the first thing I have to do is give up—surrender my life completely to you. Thank you for loving me and for giving my life meaning because of what Jesus did for me. In his name, amen.

Over the next six days, we will look at every area of our lives to see if God is truly at the center. By week's end we'll be able to decide whether we will choose to fulfill Life Choice 1 and surrender our lives completely to God.

Now that our restoration project is under way, it's time to determine if anything is interfering with our ability to hear God's voice. In our next meeting we'll spend some time retuning our ears. See you back here tomorrow!

Day 2

SURROUND SOUND

Embracing the Truth about You

Whatever is true, whatever is noble, whatever is right, whatever
is pure, whatever is lovely, whatever is admirable—
if anything is excellent or praiseworthy—
think about such things.
Philippians 4:8

God loves each of us as if there were only one of us.
—Saint Augustine

IN RECENT YEARS iPods and MP3 players have become ubiquitous, and it's not hard to see why. Music seems to take us to another world. Next time you're out and about, check out all the rock-star wannabes singing along with tunes in their cars or bopping down the street with their earbuds in place. Mentally and emotionally, these music lovers seem to enter another world, which makes them almost oblivious to the physical world they live in.

What type of tunes do you enjoy? My iPod menu holds a wide variety of tunes, with folders for rock and roll, eighties, jazz, R & B, country, and Christian worship. But the storage capacity and replay capability of these remarkable little musical hard drives are nothing compared to human memory. Have you ever played "name that tune" and guessed a favorite melody in just a few notes? It's amazing how that works. Music is definitely a gift from God.

One friend of mine has a surround-sound system in his home big enough to rival anything at Best Buy or Circuit City. You can sit in any room (even the bathroom) and hear music, which is pretty cool. The downside is that you can't go anywhere to escape it.

As I've coached people to help them become all that God made them to be, I've found that a lot of us have inner surround-sound systems playing continuously. We can't escape it, and there's no such thing as peace and quiet. But the sounds we hear are not music. Instead, they're the negative statements we've heard all our lives from other people—often a mother, father, or someone else really important to us. Their cruel messages about our looks, our abilities, our character, our potential, our value, and our lovability hound us. We start to perceive ourselves through the filter of their words and live our lives handicapped by fear and low self-worth. But these destructive messages we repeat to ourselves are flat-out *lies*.

Lies in My Head

God made our minds incredibly powerful: we can use them to calculate, solve problems, plan, recall, and store a lot of information, in addition to our favorite tunes. How good is your memory? Do you remember the two greatest goals in life? We talked about them at the beginning of this book. They're the same ones Jesus once challenged a man to remember. The man rightly answered, " 'You must love the LORD your God with all your heart, all your soul, all your strength, and all your mind.' And, 'Love your neighbor as yourself' " (Luke 10:27 NLT).

Jesus wants us to use our minds to love God. Unfortunately, most of us can't hear the truth over the noise of old messages running through our brains—over and over and over.

I remember when my counselor said to me, "Erik, what do you

listen to when the music is not playing?" He was referring to my self-talk. Here's what I wrote on the whiteboard he had on his office wall:

- Erik, you will never be able to read, write, or do math.
- Erik, you will never be good at sports.
- Erik, you constantly disappoint me.
- Erik, you will never be successful.

Those were the verbal bombs my alcoholic father had lobbed into my mind. The most hurtful one—a lie that took years to erase—was, "Erik, you'll never be anyone." I didn't hear these statements just once or twice. From when I was eight, when my parents got divorced, to when I was sixteen, when I left home, they recycled weekly—sometimes daily.

"Erik," the counselor asked, "who is the author of these sound tracks?"

Is he kidding? I thought. "My dad."

He asked me this question a second time, and I responded the same way. What didn't he get?

"No, Erik," he said. "Satan is the author of these messages, and he's trying to use your dad to destroy you." Suddenly it became clear that I was the one who didn't get it. Satan had used my dad to fill my head with lies to keep me from being who God wanted me to be. The only way to reverse a curse is to replace a lie with God's truth.

We record hurtful lies and listen to them for years on constant playback. I remember nodding as I read these words from Joyce Meyer: "I had this little recording playing in my head for years and years and years, what's wrong with me, what's wrong with me, what's wrong with me?"[1] That statement could have been mine.

Here's what the Bible says about Satan and his deceptive schemes: "He was a murderer from the beginning, not holding to the truth, for there is no truth in him. When he lies, he speaks his native language, for he is a liar and the father of lies" (John 8:44). Satan has been telling lies ever since he was kicked out of heaven. His first lie recorded in the Bible was to Eve in the Garden of Eden, when he told her it was okay to eat from the tree even though God had forbidden it. Listening to and believing lies leads to a life of bondage, which keeps us from making our lives count. Every area of oppression in our lives can be traced back to some lie we were told at some time.

The day I realized the truth—that Satan had used my dad to lie to me and keep me from being all God had made me to be—was a major turning point in my life. Although that was several years ago, I'm grateful that I can recall it when I need to—both to recognize God's goodness in my life and so I can use it to help others.

I used to think that what my dad said was how God saw me too. But that was another lie I was allowing myself to believe. No wonder Paul said that knowing God's will begins with a changed mind. His specific words were, "Do not conform any longer to the pattern of this world, but be transformed by the renewing of your mind. Then you will be able to test and approve what God's will is—his good, pleasing and perfect will" (Romans 12:2).

I had allowed my father's words to keep me focused on myself, on conforming to this self-centered world. For years I thought I was worth nothing. I made strenuous efforts to find acceptance, affirmation, and approval in all the wrong ways. But God has replaced my dad's lies with the truth of his Word. I wish I could say those old tunes no longer replay, but unfortunately they do. I thank God, though, that they don't guide my thought life anymore. When I do hear them in my head, I follow Paul's advice: "Whatever is true, whatever is noble, whatever is right, whatever is pure, whatever is lovely, whatever is admirable—if anything is excellent or praiseworthy—think about such things" (Philippians 4:8).

That's the verse my internal surround sound is founded on—my inner iTunes library, if you will. I don't waste time listening to lies anymore. I've synced with my Savior. What about you? What do you listen to when the music is not playing in your life? Does your internal surround sound mirror God's truth about you? Or are you listening to and believing Satan's lies?

Heavenly Sound Tracks

Replacing old lies with God's truth is the only thing that can free us from the deceptive bondage of Satan. Jesus declared: "The truth will set you free" (John 8:32). We need to do more than just think about God's truths—we must listen to them daily, repeat them often, memorize them, work them into the grooves in our brains and the tissue of our hearts so they can transform our beliefs and ultimately allow us to become all that God made us to be.

If listening to old lies is a problem for you, I encourage you to replace those lies with God's truth. Use this new, Scripture-based playlist that I got from my pastor and adapted to help you become all that God created you to be.

- **You're acceptable!** God says that you and I are acceptable to him. "Though my father and mother forsake me, the Lord will receive me" (Psalm 27:10).
- **You're valuable!** God says that you and I are valuable to him. "You have been bought and paid for by Christ, so you belong to him" (1 Corinthians 7:23 TLB).
- **You're lovable!** God says that you and I are lovable. " 'The mountains and hills may crumble, but my love for you will never end; I will keep forever my promise of peace.' So says the Lord who loves you" (Isaiah 54:10 GNT).
- **You're forgivable!** God says that you and I are forgivable. "I am the God who forgives your sins, and I do this because of who I am. I will not hold your sins against you" (Isaiah 43:25 GNT).
- **You're capable!** God says that you and I are capable. "I can do everything through Christ, who gives me strength" (Philippians 4:13 NLT).
- **You're usable!** God says that you and I are usable. " 'I know the plans I have for you,' declares the Lord, 'plans to prosper you and not to harm you, plans to give you hope and a future'" (Jeremiah 29:11).

- **You're special!** God says that you and I are unique—one of a kind—and extremely special to him. "We are God's masterpiece. He has created us anew in Christ Jesus, so we can do the good things he planned for us long ago" (Ephesians 2:10 NLT).

What do the sound tracks playing in your mind say about you? Are they positive and empowering or destructive and deceitful? Is there a pain from your past that distracts you? Is there a success that causes pride and disconnects you from God? We all need to inventory our lives and identify the sound tracks we hear. We can't seize the lives God has waiting for us until we surrender the things that disrupt our relationships with him.

Use the space below as I did the whiteboard in my counselor's office. List any lies or tunes of defeat you've been listening to.

Now, take those negative sound tracks to God in prayer and surrender them to him once and for all. Allow God to start renewing your mind today.

Making It Count

Sarah spent the first twenty-four years of her life defining herself by the way others saw her. Her sound tracks told her she wasn't good enough as she was, that she needed to become who others thought she should be. She was ruled by their hit parade. "I ended up not knowing who I was or what I was really like," she confessed.

Then one day God stepped in and began to turn her life around. As Sarah explains, her life now has new lyrics:

I married a man who loves me and accepts me just the way I am—quirky parts and all. I have learned to love and accept him in the same way. A counseling program has helped me strip away all the expectations others had put on me. Through it all, I have discovered that my God is bigger than I had believed him to be when I was growing up. Thanks to him, I am on the other side of the struggle. Now I know and accept who I am. Today I believe that what God says about me is true, rather than what I tell myself or how other people view me. Rather than searching everywhere for who I am, I have been in the process of believing God for who he says I am. I have realized that what God says about me is infinitely more truthful than who other people say I am. I still have details to work out in my life, but I am in the process of believing in who God says I am.

Sarah is learning to replace the old sound tracks with the beautiful music of God's love. As you reflect on Sarah's story, think about the lyrics others hear from you. What would your best friends say about the tunes you play for them? Would they say your words are cheers or criticism? What about your family? Have your words blown wind into their sails or deflated them?

The Bible calls us to encourage one another:

- "Encourage one another and build each other up, just as in fact you are doing" (1 Thessalonians 5:11).
- "Encourage one another daily, as long as it is called Today, so that none of you may be hardened by sin's deceitfulness" (Hebrews 3:13).
- "Let us consider how we may spur one another on toward love and good deeds" (Hebrews 10:24).

Are you an encourager? If this hasn't been especially true of you in the past, what can you surrender to God so that you might become an encourager, starting today? Please don't let Satan's lies rob you of the opportunity to make your unique contribution to the body of Christ—not for one more day or one more moment. Instead, focus on the promises of God.

I hope you'll spend some time today reflecting on the following verses. Learn how God really feels about you. Let his words of love replace the lies in your head. I encourage you to bookmark this page and revisit it often—even daily—until the volume of these words in your head and heart drowns out those old sound tracks.

- "As God's chosen people, holy and dearly loved, clothe yourselves with compassion, kindness, humility, gentleness and patience" (Colossians 3:12).
- "The LORD's unfailing love surrounds the man who trusts in him" (Psalm 32:10).
- "The LORD your God is with you, he is mighty to save. He will take great delight in you, he will quiet you with his love, he will rejoice over you with singing" (Zephaniah 3:17).
- "All that the Father gives me [Jesus] will come to me, and whoever comes to me I will never drive away" (John 6:37).
- "I no longer call you servants, because a servant does not know his master's business. Instead, I have called you friends, for everything that I learned from my Father I have made known to you" (John 15:15).
- "God so loved the world that he gave his one and only Son, that whoever believes in him shall not perish but have eternal life" (John 3:16).
- "Nothing can ever separate us from God's love. Neither death nor life, neither angels nor demons, neither our fears for today nor our worries about tomorrow—not even the powers of hell can separate us from God's love. No power in the sky above or in the earth below—indeed, nothing in all creation will ever be able to separate us from the love of God that is revealed in Christ Jesus our Lord" (Romans 8:38–39 NLT).

- "When you go through deep waters, I will be with you. When you go through rivers of difficulty, you will not drown. When you walk through the fire of oppression, you will not be burned up; the flames will not consume you. For I am the LORD, your God" (Isaiah 43:2–3 NLT).
- "I am the light of the world. If you follow me, you won't have to walk in darkness, because you will have the light that leads to life" (John 8:12 NLT).
- "We know that in all things God works for the good of those who love him, who have been called according to his purpose" (Romans 8:28).

You can change the sound tracks of your life when you focus on God's Word rather than on the negative messages of the world around you. Even if you've been listening to lies all your life, when you learn what God's Word says about you, it will change your life like nothing else can. At long last you'll be able to say, "Now I know who I am and why I was born." Let God's voice become your new surround-sound system. Listen to him now as you pray.

Lord, all my life I've been listening to lies. Thank you for helping me to see it! Thank you for the fact that all your words about me are words of love and not words meant to tear me down. Help me to recognize the source of those negative sound tracks playing in the background of my life, and give me the power to change the tune. I ask it in Jesus' name. . . . Amen.

Tomorrow we'll talk about how to turn our cravings over to God and let him meet our needs. Don't forget your coffee!

Day 3

CRAVINGS

Letting God Meet Your Needs

I know what it is to be in need, and I know what
it is to have plenty. I have learned the secret of being content
in any and every situation, whether well fed or hungry,
whether living in plenty or in want.
Philippians 4:12

It is better to be satisfied with what you have
than to be always wanting something else.
Ecclesiastes 6:9 GNT

If we just give God the little that we have,
we can trust Him to make it go around.
—Gloria Gaither

LIKE MOST KIDS, JAYME craved her parents' affection and attention. Her dad, however, craved alcohol. To cope with her unstable, alcoholic home, Jayme turned to food. But as a survival technique, it failed her, taking her from unhappy to almost hopeless. Jayme said, "My eating disorder destroyed my body and my life. This A-plus president of my National Honor Society, VP of student council, captain of cross-country, and softball star became a college dropout and a benchwarmer. I was tired of living a performance-driven life."

Desperate for answers, she checked into a treatment center. It was there that she heard about someone who could change her life. She recounted, "I surrendered at the feet of Jesus. Since that moment I have taken his direction for every step toward recovery. Today, because of the grace of Jesus Christ, I have a life. It's not perfect, but it is beautiful. I've learned that only Jesus can meet my needs for acceptance, affirmation, approval, and affection."

I remember a childhood much like Jayme's. Food comforted me in my pain, too, but it also gave the other kids ample ammunition to make my life even more miserable. On the grade-school playground they'd call me "Oompa-Loompa" or "Little Porker." In junior high, I made the unfortunate decision to turn to drugs. I hated how they made me feel, but they numbed the loneliness. In high school, sports became my new addiction. After all, girls loved jocks. During pregame warm-ups, I remember hoping Mom or Dad would be in the stands. Mom came to one game. Dad never did.

Today Jesus meets my needs, just as he meets Jayme's. Christ's words have brought incredible rest to my soul: "Come to me, all you who are weary and burdened, and I will give you rest. . . . For I am gentle and humble in heart, and you will find rest for your souls" (Matthew 11:28–29).

What do you crave? Does some longing in your heart gnaw at you by day and soak your pillow with tears by night? Don't let it eat you alive. In a scene at the end of *Indiana Jones and the Last Crusade,* Indiana dangles from a cliff by one hand while with the other he grasps in vain for the Holy Grail, which he and a host of others had risked life and limb to find. Taking hold of it would mean falling to his death. His father grabs Indy's wrist and softly but firmly pleads with him, "Indiana, let it go."

Whatever your holy grail is, please hear me pleading with you to let it go. Only Jesus can give you the satisfaction you seek—and he will if you come to him with your cravings and ask him to meet them for you.

I love the way the Message paraphrase translates that passage from Matthew: "Are you tired? Worn out? Burned out on religion? Come to me. Get away with me and you'll recover your life. I'll show you how to take a real rest. Walk with me and work with me—watch how I do it. Learn the unforced rhythms of grace."

Life in Christ is the path to life recovery. Jesus promises peace, and he delivers it when we seek him for that purpose.

Hungry I Come

All of us have the same basic needs for food, water, air, shelter, and security. We have a need for meaning and purpose in life. Beyond that, most people I've talked to have other, emotional needs in their lives as well. Some prefer not to acknowledge them, but they're still there. The majority of people I've coached know that they have needs: they've stopped running from them and are ready to surrender. They long to trade in their craving for true rest in the arms of Christ. Through our conversations, they come to realize that if they don't release their cravings to the Lord, those unsatisfied desires will rob them of the future God has planned for them.

Let's look at some common emotional needs people share and how they go about meeting them. More important, let's see what God says about them and how we can allow him to meet the need in our lives.

Acceptance

We all want to fit in, to be part of the group—whether it's our family, a Little League baseball team, or just our peers. It's a normal longing. When it goes unfulfilled, we might seek to fulfill it by ourselves in ways that bring damage to our lives—like joining gangs or pretending to be someone we're not.

In the parable of the lost sheep, Jesus spoke of the shepherd who left his ninety-nine sheep to go after one who was lost. Jesus said,

"When he finds it, he joyfully puts it on his shoulders and goes home. Then he calls his friends and neighbors together and says, 'Rejoice with me; I have found my lost sheep.' I tell you that in the same way there will be more rejoicing in heaven over one sinner who repents than over ninety-nine righteous persons who do not need to repent" (Luke 15:5–7).

When we belong to Jesus, he loves us that intensely. We don't need to go looking for love in all the wrong places—we just need to stay close to our shepherd. In Christ we can finally say, "I know why I'm here and where I belong."

Affirmation

We long for support from others—from our families first, and then from friends, coworkers, or, if you're running for office, from lots and lots of voters. This is another need we often seek to meet on our own in ways that can be destructive. When our families and friends fail us, we may look for approval from others we'd be better off avoiding. The Bible says, "Do not be misled: 'Bad company corrupts good character' " (1 Corinthians 15:33). So beware of making friends just to look good or to fit in with a crowd of people who might not have your best interests— or the things of God—in mind.

The Bible also reminds us, "If God is for us, who can be against us? He who did not spare his own Son, but gave him up for us all—how will he not also, along with him, graciously give us all things?" (Romans 8:31–32). You don't need to run after other things to find affirmation. God is for you! Read those verses again and again until that blessed truth sinks in: God is for you! It's a truth I and many others have come to know, and it has changed our lives. Let it change yours, too.

Approval

Who doesn't love to hear applause? I know I do. Even if we think we don't seek the limelight, the truth is that we all want to win the approval of others. But here again, we must be careful not to seek the applause of those whose only real goal is to use us for their own ends. For years I sought the applause of the corporate world. True, it did come with a lot of great perks and a nice fat paycheck. But I traded it all for the much greater rewards I've found in serving God. When we realize that God is the only audience we really need to please, we can stop striving, and our lives become much simpler. Learn to live for that audience of one, and you'll find more than a lifetime of approval. In the end, you'll hear those cherished words from the Master, "Well done." There is no greater prize.

Attention

The need for attention, to be noticed, is close to the need for approval, except that it can manifest itself negatively—in ways that draw a response quite the opposite of cheers and appreciation. Have you ever observed a two-year-old who wasn't getting her way or whose mother was ignoring her? The behavior that child often resorts to in order to get the attention she craves is rarely cute.

God wants you to know that you always have his attention. The psalmist discovered this and wrote: "Where can I go from your Spirit? Where can I flee from your presence? If I go up to the heavens, you are there; if I make my bed in the depths, you are there. If I rise on the wings of the dawn, if I settle on the far side of the sea, even there your hand will guide me, your right hand will hold me fast. If I say, 'Surely the darkness will hide me and the light become night around me,' even the darkness will not be dark to you; the night will shine like the day, for darkness is as light to you" (Psalm 139:7–12).

We all know what it's like to try to get an appointment with a high-powered person—or even our doctor. But God wants us to know that he is available to us anytime we need him. We can come to God at any moment, and he is there—ready, waiting, and willing to listen. So if it's attention you crave, surrender that longing to God. Spend time with him and bask in his presence.

Affection

I've read that the human infant cannot thrive without affection. We all need the touch of a person who loves us. Problems arise, however, when we go looking for that affection in inappropriate ways or places. It's normal for us to crave affection if it's not part of our daily home life, but God wants us to receive it in ways that build us up rather than tear us down.

"How can I get affection from God?" you may ask. Perhaps you've heard the story of the little boy who was crying, and when an adult told him to tell God his troubles, he replied, "But I need someone with skin on!" God knows we have this need: it was his idea! So if it's affection you crave, give that longing to God and wait on him. If the wait seems too long, look for ways to offer affection (in appropriate ways) to others who are craving it. Consider visiting senior centers or children's hospitals—places where people are literally dying waiting for affection. Be the answer you seek from God for someone else.

We have many other common basic needs—for conversation, companionship, encouragement, honesty, hope, security, and more. One reason we have longings is so that they will draw us to God. He allows us to have needs so that we'll go to him to have them met. In many ways, longings are what keep us hoping for heaven. God meets us where we are, but he wants us to know that life on earth will never be quite perfect. Author Kathi Macias explains it this way:

> I believe God placed that longing for home within each of us, and it's a longing that drives us throughout our lives. Sadly, most of the world's inhabitants will refuse to recognize that longing for what it really is—a homesickness for heaven and for the One who dwells there—and will therefore waste their lives trying to "plug up the hole" with other things. Whether those things consist of financial wealth or meaningful relationships or successful careers, or drugs or alcohol or crime, none will fulfill

the longing that only a personal and lasting relationship with God can produce. The Father's heart is so great and so filled with love for us that He not only provided a way for us to come home to Him by accepting His Son, Jesus, as our personal Savior, but He also calls to us daily, placing people in our paths to speak of His love and to offer the invitation to come home."[1]

Let not your hearts be troubled. Believe in God; believe also in me. In my Father's house are many rooms. If it were not so, would I have told you that I go to prepare a place for you? And if I go and prepare a place for you, I will come again and will take you to myself, that where I am you may be also.

—John 14:1–3 ESV

Making It Count

If cravings are taking you down, surrender them to the only person ever born who was tempted but never gave in. Jesus is strong when we are weak, and God's Word promises that he will never test us without giving us a way of escape: "The temptations in your life are no different from what others experience. And God is faithful. He will not allow the temptation to be more than you can stand. When you are tempted, he will show you a way out so that you can endure" (1 Corinthians 10:13 NLT).

Think of those cravings as rocks in your bucket. They're not doing you any good, not advancing you toward accomplishing the two greatest goals in life. Where you have genuine needs, let God meet them.

Otherwise, ask God to pick those rocks out of your bucket and toss them away.

Review this chapter and reflect on the cravings that have dominated your life. Write them down in the space below, and then face them.

Cravings That Dominate My Life

Recognize that resisting these cravings will not be easy. Maybe you'll need to take steps to overcome them, like finding a Celebrate Recovery[2] group at your church. I've been amazed at how many people have been helped by this life-changing ministry—not just drug addicts and alcoholics but people with all kinds of dependency issues. You can also seek the guidance of a pastor or Christian counselor in your community.

Finally, surrender your cravings to God. Ask him to meet your deepest longings and bring you his amazing peace. It may not happen overnight, but if you keep pursuing him, in time you'll find that the hold those cravings have over your life will diminish . . . until one day they may just disappear altogether. Let's ask him for his help right now.

Lord, thank you for helping me to see how these things I thought I needed were controlling my life. In reality, you are all I really need! Now that I have you in my life, I can trust you to supply the rest. Give me the courage to let go of anything that stands in the way of a life totally surrendered to you. In Jesus' sweet name, amen!

When we meet over coffee tomorrow, we'll grapple with those rocks other people have thrown at us that have left scars and scrapes. Believe it or not, through God even those can have a purpose.

SCRAPES AND SCARS

Healing Old Wounds

Forgetting what is behind and straining toward
what is ahead, I press on toward the goal to win the prize
for which God has called me heavenward in Christ Jesus.
Philippians 3:13–14

Pain is temporary. It may last a minute, or an hour,
or a day, or a year, but eventually it will subside and something
else will take its place. If I quit, however, it lasts forever.
—Lance Armstrong

BY THE AGE OF twenty-five, he had it made. Already a world-class cyclist, he had a custom-built home with a pool, drove a Porsche, and had at least $2.5 million in signed contracts to keep him busy for a while. But something was wrong. Even racing fans noticed it when, after winning the 1996 Tour DuPont, he failed to give his signature fist-pumping victory sign. Instead, he seemed riddled with pain. Lance Armstrong was about to find out how quickly life can change.

"One minute you're pedaling along a highway, and the next minute, *boom,* you're facedown in the dirt," Armstrong wrote of his diagnosis with testicular cancer. "It was like being run off the road by a truck, and I've got the scars to prove it."[1] Today he is a cancer survivor and record-holding seven-time winner of bicycling's World Cup—the Tour de France. His life is, in some ways, inspirational. Armstrong knows what happens if we let life's pain take us out of the race, and he's determined not to let that happen. If we live in the past, the pain never goes away and we learn nothing to take with us into the future.

Where do you live? I'm not talking about your physical home but how you view life. A survey I once heard about indicated that 50 percent of people live their lives looking back at the past, while 40 percent live in the moment and 10 percent live their lives thinking about the future. In which era are you spending most of your time? Are you stuck in the past, stewing about the pain, injustices, and sorrows of yesterday? What a painful exercise in futility! It's time to learn something from your dog. Renowned dog trainer Cesar Millan says dogs live in the moment. I believe that God wants us to let go of the past, set our hopes on the future, but train ourselves to live, like all those wise dogs, in the present.

Surrendering Your Scrapes and Scars

Lance Armstrong understands that physical pain does not go away without concerted effort on our part to get well. It's the same with wounds of the heart. God longs for you to trust him with those things that have brought you great pain. He'll do the healing, but you've got to bring him your hurts—and for many of us that takes great effort. But I've learned from my life and witnessed in the lives of many others that when we are faithful to do that first part, God does the rest. Let him heal the fresh, open wounds until they are nothing more than faded scars, useful only for helping you understand the pain of others. Even if you believe the damage is irreparable, Scripture says that God is able to mend it: "He heals the brokenhearted and binds up their wounds" (Psalm 147:3).

One of God's many titles is the Great Physician. He's in the business of healing our wounds—both the physical and the emotional injuries we've sustained. Where have you been hurt? Tell God about it and let the healing begin.

In spite of my difficult childhood, I am stunned by the emotional scars carried by so many young people. Not long ago I received a list of wounds borne by teenagers who had talked about them in a group setting. They shared their biggest problems and how they dealt with them. Their stories pulled me into prayer for each young soul; as they spoke of the pain caused by divorce, new schools, no friends, incest, physical and emotional abuse, it broke my heart.

What pressure—and before they're even adults with the maturity to deal with these issues! It was particularly sad to notice how many of these kids were suffering as a result of choices made by the adults in their lives.

The different ways in which teens deal with problems reflect how we as adults still react to troubles. Understandably, some teens' responses are healthier than others'. Those who ignore their pressures and problems, sadly, are only burying their pain. Unless they deal with that pain, one day it will resurface. But some in the study said they were praying about their problems. These will hopefully discover that Christ is their ultimate answer. Perhaps then they'll help lead their friends to the same conclusion. If any of these stories sounds like yours, may you in time learn to see life through God's eyes. No one has suffered more pain and injustice than Jesus did, so you can be sure that he understands.

The LORD is close to the brokenhearted and
saves those who are crushed in spirit.
—Psalm 34:18

Knowing that Jesus suffered as we do and understands our problems goes a long way toward giving us confidence to surrender our scars and hurts to God. But how do we actually do that—give it to Jesus—and begin the healing process? It all starts with forgiveness. Forgiveness goes both ways: we must be able to give as well as receive forgiveness. Not only must we decide to forgive those who have wounded us, but we must also forgive ourselves for doing things that hurt God or others, and we must ask God to forgive us. Forgiveness is no light matter to God. Listen to what Jesus told Peter when it sounded like he was looking for an excuse not to forgive: "Peter came to him and asked, 'Lord, how often should I forgive someone who sins against me? Seven times?' 'No, not seven times,' Jesus replied, 'but seventy times seven!'" (Matthew 18:21–22 NLT).

I'm not saying that you have to forget the pain a person caused you. You'll likely never forget it. It's not about minimizing the offense, instantly restoring trust, or picking up in the relationship as if nothing had happened. Just as a physical scar endures, you'll probably always have a scar on your heart where you were wounded. But forgiveness is an essential part of setting yourself free.

If someone has hurt you deeply, please realize that holding on to bitterness toward that person actually hurts *you*. You need to forgive the person who wounded you—not for his or her sake but for your own. I know that may sound impossible—it did to me when I realized that I needed to forgive my dad. But with God's help—and only with God's help—it is possible. Forgiveness is your part of surrendering the scars and scrapes.

Divorce, alcoholism, cancer, financial stress, feelings of not being loved or wanted, loneliness, infidelity, life-threatening illnesses, eating disorders, pornography, imprisonment, abuse from others: these are not just problems you picked up as an adult. The roots run deep, often stretching back many years to seeds of destruction planted in your childhood or youth. You may have deep pain that's been part of your life for such a long time that you don't know how to let it go.

Depending on your situation, you may need to go to the person who inflicted these wounds and forgive him or her, or you may need to ask for forgiveness from that person. If that's not possible, then ask God to give you the strength to forgive—and then live as though you mean it. Forgiveness is instant; restoration takes time. Don't allow that pain from your past to cripple you one moment longer.

Amy, whose story we'll read more of in Day 7, shared this about her process of healing with God: "The difficult part has been acceptance of my life—the painful circumstances, the grief of loss—and being able to forgive those who caused the unnecessary hurt I experienced. What amazes me every day is how God has used those bad times to uniquely shape me into the person I am today."

God wants to use your pain, your grief, and your scars and scrapes, too. I encourage you to face those scrapes and scars by writing them down in the space below. Something about looking at them in print brings them out of hiding and into the light, where they have a chance to heal.

You may be tempted to think, *Oh, my problems aren't such a big deal.* But anything that keeps you from fully being the you God intended is a big deal to God. Ask him to reveal to you any old hurts that are hindering your development.

If you've suffered serious emotional injury at the hands of another, I encourage you to seek professional help from a Christian counselor. Only you can be you, but if old scars or scrapes are in your way, you've got to surrender them to God by forgiving those who've hurt you.

Surrendering Your Guilt

Most scars are caused by others, but we harbor guilt when we've been the ones to cause the scars or when we've accepted the lies of the accuser. We don't like to admit when we've been wrong, but if we don't, our guilt tends to grow and grow until it's so big that we become blind to it.

At that point, we justify our actions rather than admit we're wrong, no matter who gets hurt in the process.

> There is no condemnation
> for those who belong to Christ Jesus.
> Romans 8:1 NLT

Few things stall the process of becoming the real you more than guilt. For starters, we must realize that guilt never comes from God. But our enemy, the devil, delights in our guilt. He encourages it and whispers to us that we deserve it.

Guilt is never productive. It only hurts—and hurts and hurts—and it ripples outward to affect everyone in our path. It causes great sorrow with no good end: self-condemnation, shame, remorse, regret.

But this doesn't have to be the end when we've done wrong. The Bible talks about another kind of sorrow—the kind that leads to a changed heart and a new direction. This kind of sorrow leads us to repentance. I like to think of repenting as turning around and going the other way.

God's Word *convicts* us of sin. Unlike guilt, conviction is productive. It leads us to confess what we've done wrong. When we do, God is faithful to forgive us. He promises in 1 John 1:9 that "if we confess our sins, he is faithful and just and will forgive us our sins and purify us from all unrighteousness."

Conviction is the key to being set free. If you're feeling guilty about something you've already surrendered to Christ, you can be sure Satan is simply playing on your past, scraping away at the old scars. The moment you confessed it, God forgot it. But if you are carrying guilt that needs your confession and repentance, don't put it off one more moment.

Judas put it off. Here was a man who had walked with Jesus and learned at his feet. Yet he was being dishonest, and he knew it. He was stealing money from the ministry's funds—money that had been donated to help the poor (John 12:6). Judas didn't admit his guilt; he denied it. He hid it until it had grown so big that it caused him to betray Jesus himself. Once the act had been committed, Judas was sorry—but instead of surrendering his guilt, he let it chase him to the point where he took his own life. Once the high priests had what they wanted, Judas could go hang himself for all they cared. And so he did . . . his guilt intact and unforgiven.

> I had lots of hurt and lots of pain, lots of woundedness, bruises, brokenheartedness in my life. I was abused sexually by my father, abused mentally, emotionally. My mom didn't know what to do about it, and she was being hurt in the process. So she just didn't deal with it. And I can guarantee you, just because you don't deal with something, that doesn't make it go away.
> —Joyce Meyer

Don't be like Judas. If guilt has you hung up, confess it! God already knows what you've done, but until you confess it to him, you'll never be free from its poison. Let it out, confess it, and know what it feels like to be free at last.

Making It Count

I've found that all people wear masks to one degree or another to hide their emotional scars. I'm not talking about a physical mask but the imaginary mask known only to the person wearing it. We can become so used to our game of hideaway that we're not even aware we have the masks on. They allow us to temporarily relieve an inner longing by pretending to be someone we're not. The mask of importance is put on to make an insecure person look secure. The mask of materialism helps the lonely person feel valued. The mask of security helps the fearful person look strong. And the peaceful mask helps the worrier look calm. These masks allow us to hide from reality, but they really don't help us at all. In fact, they usually compound our problems.

Some people wear masks to get attention. The know-it-all mask helps the lonely person feel important. The bully mask helps the weak feel strong. The wealthy mask helps people feel outwardly rich, when inside they are poor.

God isn't fooled by our masks. In fact, the only people we end up fooling are ourselves. Here's one of the many ways in which the Bible contrasts the wise with the foolish: "The wise inherit honor, but fools he holds up to shame" (Proverbs 3:35). Which future do you look forward to?

You don't need to pretend. You're valuable to God just the way you are. He made you, and he knows all about your imperfections. He actually planned them to be a part of you so that through them you could grow to be like his Son.

Today I want you to reflect on the scars and scrapes in your life.

- In what areas are you being held captive by an old scar?
- What scrapes have you caused in another person's life?
- Where do you need God's power to forgive or to turn your life around?
- Who needs to hear, "Please forgive me," from your lips?
- What masks have you been hiding behind?

Why not let God reveal the true you, a person he loves so much that he gave his own Son to save you? Take an honest inventory of your life, and use the space below to write down your thoughts.

Now place your list of scars and scrapes at the foot of God's throne, throw yourself on his mercy, and feel the fountain of his grace wash over your life. Let's do that together.

Lord, help me to see not the person other people have told me I am but the person you say I am. I don't have the strength to forgive the person or people who have hurt me, but I believe that you can forgive them through me. What's more, you've helped me understand that my failure to forgive doesn't hurt them at all—in the end, it only hurts me. I long to live a life that's whole and strong and purposeful, not crippled by my past. Set me free, Father, by your power. Show me what you need me to do, and give me the strength to do it. By the power of Jesus I pray, amen!

Purify me from my sins, and I will be clean;
wash me, and I will be whiter than snow.
Psalm 51:7 NLT

Now that we've surrendered the wounds caused by others, we'll take on releasing to God the other people and relationships so important in our lives. See you back here tomorrow.

Day 5

TODAY

Releasing Your Roles and Relationships

This is the confidence we have in approaching God:
that if we ask anything according to his will, he hears us.
And if we know that he hears us—whatever we ask—
we know that we have what we asked of him.
1 John 5:14–15

Stress is the trash of modern life—we all generate it but if you
don't dispose of it properly, it will pile up and overtake your life.
Danzae Pace

ALARM CLOCKS, DEAD BATTERIES, traffic jams, ringing phones, long lines, crying babies, deadlines, bills piling up . . . how do *you* spell stress?

If we tried to identify one worldwide, unifying characteristic of human life, I suspect it would be living in anxiety, or, as we call it today, stress. People seem to be stressed out over so many things these days.

For some, stress comes on occasionally, when prompted by extraordinary circumstances. Many others, however, are chronic worriers. They spend their days stewing and fretting over all the things they want to control or fix but cannot. After a while, carrying the constant weight of our burdens drags us down and distances us from God.

What concerns cause you stress and rob you of today's joy? Is it the roles you play, the relationships in your life, your finances, your future—what? You can shout, "Hakuna matata!" (meaning "no worries") all you want, but if worrying is in your nature or if cares have gotten you down, that cute little phrase will do nothing to solve your problems. So what can you do?

Giving God Your Roles

So you want to be you, but you're confused by all the roles you play. Five days a week you're your job, and the rest of the time (what little there is) you're a mom or a dad or a soccer-game chauffeur or a volunteer traffic director at church. You feel like screaming, "Who am I, anyway?"

Phil Vischer dreamed of becoming the next Walt Disney. He began his company, Big Idea, with a longing to send a godly message to children through films. What could be more pure? And it worked! His *Veggie Tales* animated films were wildly successful. But because he'd pushed so hard to make his dream come true, ultimately his life began to fall apart. "It was affecting my health, my marriage, my kids, my employees. I was increasingly miserable, run-down, burned out . . . pushing a rock uphill."

And then Phil's dream died. "In hindsight," he said, "it was a divine mercy killing. He [God] stood back and let my dream fall apart. I saw that it wasn't what I needed, and that my fulfillment comes not from anything I dream up or pull off with my own power."[1]

By releasing his role to God, Phil is rebuilding his life under God's direction. He's learning that he can be only who God made him to be. That's the message God wants you to get, too: only you can be you. So if you're wrestling with roles that don't fulfill you or you're trying to push yourself into a place where you don't belong, give up! Before you run into that wall, put on the brakes and ask God to direct you into his plan for your life. You may find yourself totally surprised by what he has in mind, but when you get there, you'll see that it's exactly where you belong.

My wife, Stacey, is incredibly gifted. During this present season of her life, as a mom of three very active kids, she sometimes feels she's not doing what God made her to do. But she's serving exactly where God wants her right now. When he's ready to move her on, the doors will open for her to explore new territory.

If you are in a season in which you feel God has you on a shelf, or you're feeling frustrated with a position that seems not quite right for you, I hope you can realize that there are many roles God has for you to fill throughout your lifetime. A few years ago I heard Pastor Francis Chan speak about thinking of ourselves as extras in God's movie. What a great image! If you place your trust in God, consult him daily, and follow his lead, you'll be playing exactly the roles he has in mind for you—each one designed to help you become a little more like his Son.

In 1 Peter 5:7 we are told to cast all our cares on the Lord, because he cares for us. When I think about the word *cast,* I picture a heaving or tossing. Whenever you find yourself worried about the roles you play, heave those concerns onto God. He knows what they are, and he knows what you need to be doing. When you talk to him about your roles, in time you'll see what he sees: the you only you can be.

Of all the roles we play, some bring fulfillment and others bring frustration. Most likely, everything we do has a little of both aspects; but one quality will generally outweigh the other. For example, one of my current roles is that of daddy. On most days it brings me great joy. Yet on some days it pushes my frustration to heights I wouldn't have believed possible. Kids have an amazing talent for bringing out the ugliness in their parents. We want them to be a certain way or behave a specific way because it makes our lives easier. When our frustrations run high, maybe we're the ones who need to take a mental time-out to check our emotions and motives. Nothing helps quite as much as holding on to a promise of God, like the one in Proverbs 3:5, to get you through those storms: "Trust in the LORD with all your heart and lean not on your own understanding; in all your ways acknowledge him, and he will make your paths straight." The best place to be at those frustrating times is at the feet of Jesus, surrendering the roles we've assumed on our own and asking for divine wisdom and strength.

Financial stress has huge influence over the roles we choose today. We often settle for a job that pays the bills rather than one that offers personal and professional growth opportunities. Bill worked for a company that paid him top dollar for his technical expertise. He could afford almost anything he wanted, but inside he just wasn't satisfied. When a chance came his way to use those skills for his church, he took the risk even though it meant that his income would take a steep nosedive. Through it all, Bill has learned to trust God to provide for his needs. He has learned the truth that only you can be you, and he's loving every minute of his life doing what God made him to do.

What about your roles? Which ones are most fulfilling? In the first column below, list the roles you currently have. Next to each one, in the second column, indicate whether that role primarily brings you fulfillment or frustration. Use this time to celebrate these roles and praise God for the fulfillment they bring to your life. Then look at any roles that are causing frustration, and use this time to surrender them to God. Are you working in a job you love or one you need just to pay the bills? Thank him for the frustrating roles as well, as each one helps you discern more of God's will for your life. Ask for his divine wisdom regarding your roles, and he will give it to you. It's another of his promises: "If you need wisdom, ask our generous God, and he will give it to you. He will not rebuke you for asking" (James 1:5 NLT).

My Current Roles   **Fulfillment or Frustration?**

Giving God Your Relationships

The other day I received an email that began, "God determines who walks into your life . . . it's up to you to decide whom you let walk away, whom you let stay, and whom you refuse to let go." That is so true. Relationships are not like loaves of bread in a supermarket. We don't get to walk in, look over a choice of people, and decide, "I'll take that one." Some relationships are determined in advance, like the family we're born into, while others are determined as we go through life. Friends come our way largely as a matter of geography—where we live, where we work, where we go to school. And often it's in those places that we also meet the one who may become our spouse.

No matter how or where those connections develop, we need to recognize that God brings them into our lives. Recognizing that he has a divine purpose for connecting us with each person in our lives can radically change how we view our relationships. Even though I was an adult long before this concept sank in, I now understand that even my relationship with my father can be used by God to bring glory to his name. I am who I am today largely because of that childhood: I notice people more, I care for people more, and I listen to people more than I might if not for that experience. Learn to see your relationships in this light. Surrender the impact of those people—both the tender and the toxic—to God, and you will witness amazing transformations in your life.

Maggie's marriage was in serious trouble. Having failed at marriage before, her feelings of anguish as she watched another relationship spiraling out of control gripped her heart and sent her reeling. This was her Christian marriage, the one she and her husband had dedicated to God. How could it go wrong? Daily she asked God why, but her heart was far from God. "I wasn't happy," she said. "I didn't understand why this man and this marriage were failing me. By the time he expressed willingness to go to counseling, I was ready to walk out.

"In time, God spoke to my heart and told me I needed to be willing, too. He turned me around and helped me see life through his eyes. It's amazing what can happen when we choose to live God's way." Living

God's way isn't always easy, but when we surrender even our difficult relationships to him, he can bring us victory.

Seth and Vanessa faced another kind of surrender where their son Jude was concerned. When Jude was just seven months old, his parents learned that he has a rare disease called tuberous sclerosis complex (TSC), a genetic disorder that, according to one website, "causes tumors to form in many different organs, primarily in the brain, eyes, heart, kidney, skin and lungs."[2] The disease manifests itself in epileptic-like seizures and can inhibit all areas of development. As painful as this diagnosis was to hear, Seth and Vanessa recognized that God had given them this precious little boy. As they acknowledge God's total control over Jude's life and future and lean on God daily, recommitting Jude to him every day, Seth and Vanessa are witnessing great progress in their son's development.

> I would have lost heart, unless I had believed
> that I would see the goodness of the LORD
> in the land of the living.
> Psalm 27:13 NKJV

They are still in the middle of what Seth calls a "very trying storm," with Jude facing surgery to control his seizures. God alone knows what Jude's future holds. His parents know this, so they have released him into God's care.

God does not promise us "happily ever after" in any relationship. But God is developing us to live happily ever after in heaven. To get ready for that, we must learn to get along with others here on earth. That means continually surrendering our relationships to God. Sometimes that means doing the hard thing because it's the right thing.

Whom will you let walk away or stay? Whom will you refuse to let go? Is it a spouse, a child, a coworker, a friend? Which relationships are causing you anxiety or heartache? Whom do you need to thank God for in your life? I hope you'll take a few moments right now to identify those relationships in the space below. Thank God for bringing them into your life, and ask him to direct them. It's not something you can do once and it's accomplished: you'll undoubtedly need to return to God's throne room on a regular basis. The good news is, his door is always open.

Thank you, Lord, for these key relationships in my life. I surrender them all to you today.

Giving God Your Day, Every Day

When we worry about the future, we're wasting today. God gives us each day so that we can give it back to him in service.

Cynthia Briggeman worried about her baby, and she worried about how she was going to get any sleep. Her infant daughter cried day and night. Grateful to have her husband there for support, she paced the floor with little Alexis, thinking about all the people whose moms or dads, husbands or wives, or sons or daughters could not be with them because they're in Iraq or Afghanistan putting their lives on the line for their fellow American citizens.

Rather than waste those often-sleepless nights, Cynthia opted to become proactive on behalf of kids whose parents are away serving in the military. She researched the U.S. Marine Corps–sponsored Toys for Tots and came up with a program of her own. In Pack for the Future, Cynthia and other volunteers fill backpacks with school supplies and a red, white, or blue teddy bear. Since 2005 they've given more than two thousand backpacks a year to kids at military bases in Southern California. Cynthia learned how to turn her concern into welcome appreciation for the sacrifice of others.[3]

> You can think about your problems
> or you can worry about them, and there is
> a vast difference between the two. Worry
> is thinking that has turned toxic. . . . The
> problem of life is to change worry into
> thinking and anxiety into creative action.
> —Harold B. Walker

God wants to use you, too. But if you're stewing over finances or business problems or relationships, or any other problems that are largely out of your hands, you can't be effective for God or anyone else right now—and you're wasting your time. God will use anything we place in his hands to bless others and glorify him. It flies in the face of human logic, but the fact is, God wants to use all of us. The only thing that stops him is our unwillingness to give him the raw material—us. God won't violate the free will he has given us.

In his letter to the church at Ephesus, Paul addressed the human tendency to waste time: "Don't waste your time on useless work, mere busywork, the barren pursuits of darkness. Expose these things for the sham they are. It's a scandal when people waste their lives on things they must do in the darkness where no one will see. Rip the cover off those frauds and see how attractive they look in the light of Christ. Wake up from your sleep, climb out of your coffins; Christ will show you the light! So watch your step. Use your head. Make the most of every chance you get. These are desperate times! Don't live carelessly, unthinkingly. Make sure you understand what the Master wants" (Ephesians 5:11–17 MSG).

If you'll be honest with yourself for a moment, you'll acknowledge that worrying about tomorrow is a barren pursuit of darkness. When you worry, you're wasting time. Admit it! What problems are you solving when you worry?

Release those things that occupy your mind by listing them below, and then hand that list to God. Let him amaze you. Let Christ bring you into the light and show you how to treasure each day and live it fully, unhampered by issues you can't control.

Things That Occupy My Mind

Making It Count

I'd like you to reflect today on those things we've discussed—your roles, relationships, and greatest concerns. God wants you to surrender these to him—everything—every day of your life. As you do, remember to thank him for those things in your life that are good or even great. God inhabits the praises of his people. Developing an attitude of gratitude will take you a long way down the road of learning to be you.

Will you pray with me?

Thank you, Lord, for showing me that although the roles and relation-ships in my life have not always been what I would choose for myself, they are all a part of your great plan for my life. Both the good and the not so good serve your purpose. As the story of Joseph tells us in Genesis 50:20, what others might mean for evil, you can turn to good. Help me, God, to always be grateful for what you bring into my life and to look expectantly to you for what you will bring out of it. In Jesus' name, amen.

Robyn takes time every night to write in her gratitude journal. She thinks back on her day and records at least five things for which she is grateful. The next morning she reads back over that notation and praises God for his goodness. What a great way to start the day. When you focus on the wonder and majesty of God, the stress in your life can't help but melt away. Even great coffee can't do that.

Speaking of coffee, tomorrow we'll meet here again to talk over what happens when we surrender our dreams and desires to God. How can something so intangible be so hard to relinquish? Yet, this can be the biggest challenge of them all.

Day 6

DREAMS AND DESIRES

Surrendering All Your Tomorrows

*I heard the Lord asking, "Whom should I send as a messenger to
this people? Who will go for us?" I said, "Here I am. Send me."*
Isaiah 6:8 NLT

*There are those who have a life they never live. They have come
to Christ and thanked Him only for what He did,
but do not live in the power of who He is.*
—Major W. Ian Thomas, Torchbearers International

PAULINE HAD BEEN ACTIVE in the church for many years. She was
happy enough, but her Christian life was not especially dynamic.
Deep inside, she knew there should be more. One night, at a church
service, her heart was stirred by a challenge to surrender her future
to God. Not long afterward, she was asked to lead a ministry at her
church. "I didn't say no, even though that's what was on my mind,"
Pauline confessed. Today she is leading studies, writing material for
her ministry, and training new leaders. "I have learned to fly and feel
fulfilled," she said, "always looking for what God would require of me
next."

Now that you've given God your past—the clutter in your life, the
old sound tracks, your cravings, the scars and scrapes, your roles and re-

lationships—it's time to trust him with tomorrow. Can you do that? It may seem scary in the beginning, like the first time you rode your bike without training wheels. But think of God as the strong, loving adult who was there to catch you if you fell. He won't send you anywhere he hasn't already gone first, and his everlasting arms are always undergirding you. Where is God nudging you to go? Maybe it's time to take those training wheels off.

Giving God Your Dreams and Desires

God knows what you long for. He knows your deepest desires and wishes. It's likely that in some way, they were his idea. Whatever dream you hold dearest was most likely planted there by God, but it needs to be given back to him before you can actually know what it's supposed to look like. When seen through God's eyes, your dream takes on clarity and purpose. He'll show you which elements of your dream are from him and which part is from your own selfishness and needs to be discarded. At long last you'll begin to see your dream's eternal value.

Only you can be you, so if you want to make your life count, you'll need to trust God a little more every day. When you do, the path he has planned for you will become clearer.

Trust in the LORD with all your heart;
do not depend on your own understanding.
Seek his will in all you do,
and he will show you which path to take.
Proverbs 3:5–6 NLT

I never run out of dreams—dreams for myself, dreams for my family, dreams for my friends, dreams for my church . . . the list goes on. But I must always remember to check my heart with God to make sure my dreams are what he desires, too, not just what I want. It should be the same way for all of us.

On the night before he went to the cross, Jesus prayed a prayer that should become our model. In the garden of Gethsemane, three times he prayed, "My Father, if it is possible, may this cup be taken from me. Yet not as I will, but as you will" (Matthew 26:39). Yes, even Jesus had dreams and a natural will to live and avoid suffering. But we can thank God that Jesus' desire to please his father was stronger than any human longing he may have had. As we can see from Jesus' example, not every dream God has for us is free of considerable sacrifice or pain. In spite of this, God's plan is always his ultimate best for us.

I'm grateful that my wife, Stacey, is alert to those times when the angle of my desires is a little too inward. Trusted friends are great motivation checkers, too. Ask yourself, "Who is the primary beneficiary of this wish?" If it turns out it's only you, look for ways to divert your attention from that longing. In time it will fade. It's not that personal desires are bad in and of themselves; it's just that they take our attention away from what matters most in favor of benefits that are short term at best. We've got to keep our eyes on the two greatest goals in life: to love God and to love others. The best way to be sure you're on the right track is to ask God himself. In James 1:5 we're told: "If any of you lacks wisdom, he should ask God, who gives generously to all without finding fault, and it will be given to him." God knows what we need. Jesus told us: "Seek first his kingdom and his righteousness and all these things will be given to you as well" (Matthew 6:33).

I have held many things in my hands, and I have lost them all; but whatever I have placed in God's hands, that I still possess.
—Martin Luther

Total surrender can be intimidating, as Michael learned a few years ago. He'd spent more than twenty years with one of the largest oil and gas companies in America, using his doctorate in business administration to achieve success. But inside, he just wasn't finding the freedom and fulfillment he longed for. He had dreamed of serving God in ministry for years. What was he supposed to be doing? How could he make his life count? Was this job it? Michael was not convinced. "Then I took a position as worship and discipleship pastor at my local church," Michael said. "The job came with about a two-thirds cut in pay. The bonuses alone I'd been making for the gas company are close to what I now make as a salary. But I'd learned that I was made to do something different from what I'd been doing, so I took that step of faith, believing God could take care of the details." Michael is learning that only he can be Michael, and at long last he is finding that freedom and fulfillment. And God has been taking care of the details.

What do you dream about? Ask God to help you clarify your dreams and take one step closer to living the life that counts.

Letting Go

When the prophet Isaiah received his assignment from God, it was accompanied by an odd promise. First, God told Isaiah to go and deliver his message of hope; then he told him that he would harden the hearts of Isaiah's audience to the message (Isaiah 6:9–10). Talk about being set up to fail! Isaiah easily could have been discouraged by this dismal forecast, yet he obeyed God all the same. This is what it means to be a faithful servant: you do as God directs and leave the results up to him. It could be that you will not see the fruit of your dreams in your lifetime; but, like Isaiah, you need to learn to think eternally. As Paul wrote to the church at Colosse, "Since, then, you have been raised with Christ, set your hearts on things above, where Christ is seated at the right hand of God. Set your minds on things above, not on earthly things. For you died, and your life is now hidden with Christ in God. When Christ, who is your life, appears, then you also will appear with him in glory" (Colossians 3:1–4).

The decision to let go of your dreams forces you to look deep into your soul. That can hurt—a lot. But just as we find new freedom when we confess our failures to God and ask for forgiveness, so it is when we release our dreams and hopes. When we give them to God with our hands wide open—when we uncurl our fingers and unclench our fists and release our dreams—for the first time in our lives, we can enjoy freedom of mind, body, and soul. We can stop competing and comparing and start contributing solely for him. And God is finally free to begin completing his masterpiece in our lives. It's as if you can hear him say, "Ahhhh. This is the moment I've been waiting for."

If you've never had your surrender moment, do it now. Don't be afraid of taking this important step, and don't listen to Satan's lie that you don't need to do it. The Bible assures us that the only thing we are to fear is God: "Do not fear anything except the Lord Almighty. He alone is the Holy One. If you fear him, you need fear nothing else. He will keep you safe" (Isaiah 8:13–14 NLT). Step out in faith. Then do whatever it takes to make sure you remain surrendered to God. One way to do this is by sharing your commitment with a close friend or family member and making yourselves accountable to each other. Or pray along with new believers every time a prayer of faith is spoken in church. Start out each day by saying, "Lord, I give you this day in my life and all that is in it. Let all that I do and every thought in my mind be pleasing to you. May the activities of my day bring you glory."

The point is, once you surrender, don't ever retreat. Yes, you may have moments when you wonder if God is really there. He is. It wouldn't be faith if it weren't tested now and again. But through it all, as long as you remain yielded to God, you can count on him to show up.

Nick Vujicic didn't want to let go of his bitterness. And who could blame him? For no apparent medical reason, Nick had been born with no arms or legs. What kind of loving God would allow a child to be born like this? What kind of life could a man with no arms or legs expect to have? How in the world would he live?

"I was definitely angry with God when I was eight years old," Nick told journalist Dan Wooding, "and I didn't really want anything to do with God. I felt like He owed me an explanation of why He did this to me. Between the ages of eight and twelve I really didn't see much hope to my life, and over the journey of my childhood, I was often thinking of how to commit suicide."

Nick was a man who had plenty of clutter: a head full of old, lying tunes; a longing to be "normal"; a past that made no sense whatsoever; no real identity; and a lifetime of scars. In short, he felt he had no reason to go on.

"But at the age of fifteen, I read in John chapter nine, where a man was born blind. Jesus was asked why this man was born blind and He said it was done so that the 'works of God may be revealed through him' and, as I read this, a wave of faith and peace came over me. I realized that no one knew why that man was born blind and no one knew why I was born this way, but Jesus did and Jesus does know why He did this to me—so that the 'works of God maybe [sic] revealed.'"

> The most dramatic realization was that in surrender I would find more freedom and power than I'd ever known.
> —Brett Butler

That revelation has led Nick to a full-time ministry through which he is spreading hope and purpose to audiences around the world. As he travels, he shares his story at churches, in small groups, or wherever he can find entry.

"I believe we all have disabilities," he said, "whether it's a physical disability or fear or guilt. Fear or guilt will hold you back more than the loss of arms and legs. . . . I don't know your pain and God is the only one that can tell you the two things that your soul longs to hear: number one that you are loved and number two, everything's going to be ok [sic]."[1]

If Nick Vujicic can look at his future and say that everything's going to be okay, what do the rest of us have to worry about? Nick has let go of the ideas he once had about life—that he should have arms and legs like everyone else—and given his life back to God. And through his life, God is being glorified.

God wants to use your life in that way, too. You may not end up traveling the world or serving in a global ministry, but your life can and will have eternal significance if you surrender it to God. What's your alternative? You can hold on to your hopes, dreams, goals, plans—your life—and burn up a few more hours serving nothing but selfishness. But what's the point of that? I pray that you will not only consider the fully surrendered life but that you will begin living it today—right this minute.

In that moment that you surrender all to God for the first time, you'll begin to discover the you he meant you to be—the you that only you can be. I say "for the first time" because surrendering to God is something we must do continually, since our human tendency is to act as if we were only kidding. Surrender must become a way of life.

My hope is that our first week together has helped you to realize what singer/songwriter Chris Tomlin expressed so well in his song "Made to Worship." In the lyrics, Tomlin hints that when we embrace surrender, when we choose to believe—*then* we will see who God made us to be.

Making It Count

Remember that analogy about God being like the strong adult who would catch you if you fell off your bike? After a time, when you've seen God's faithfulness over and over again, trusting him becomes a little less like taking off without the security of training wheels. When you reach that point—get ready. For at that time you can be sure that you're ready for a new challenge. But God is trustworthy, and his grace is endless.

Today, reflect on those dreams you've cherished all your life. Are you ready to let them go? List them in the space below as a way to make them real. What have you really got to lose?

Tell God that you want to live the life for which he created you. Ask him to reveal to you those areas you've been holding on to just for yourself and to show you how he wants to turn them inside out. Here's a great visual aid from my friend Pastor Buddy Owens:

- Hold the list in your hands, and hold it up toward heaven in a gesture of offering.
- Next, turn your hands palm downward, letting the list fall to the floor, to symbolize letting go.
- Finally, turn your hands upward again in praise and worship to God. Thank him for what he is about to do in your life.

Let's offer this prayer together.

Lord, thank you for helping me to see that you created me for a purpose. I long to live the life you've created me to live. Reveal to me those areas I've been selfishly holding on to, and show me how I can offer them to others in order to find freedom and fulfillment. I recognize this desire as having been planted in my heart by you and given fresh life through Jesus Christ, in whose name I pray. Amen.

Let's meet back here tomorrow, and we'll review what it means to live the fully surrendered life. Think of it as moving day! When you finally surrender everything to God, it's like leaving all your old junk behind and moving into a brand-new place.

Day 7

MOVING DAY
Getting a Fresh Start with God

Look! I stand at the door and knock.
If you hear my voice and open the door, I will come in,
and we will share a meal together as friends.
—Jesus Christ (Revelation 3:20 NLT)

In order to make a fresh start, we need to be willing to let go of
what lies behind and take hold of what lies ahead. I believe that
some of the most important areas where all of us need a fresh
start are how we see ourselves, how we think that God sees us,
and what we see before us in our future.
—Joyce Meyer

LONG BEFORE MY FAMILY restored that fireplace we talked about on Day 1, there was moving day. We were thrilled about our new house, but after weeks of planning and packing, signing papers, and biting our nails waiting for escrow to close, we were covered with dust, on edge, and worn out. Surrounded by boxes on moving day, Stacey and I surveyed the rooms full of stuff still to go. Blowing her hair out of her face, Stacey said, "Can't we just toss it all and start over?" Oh, how I wanted to shout, "Yes!" But when we finally got into our new home and had everything put away, the joy we felt erased all the weariness. It was as if we'd been renewed. There's something about a new home that says "fresh start."

When God comes into our lives, he offers us that opportunity—a chance to start clean. In Psalm 103:12 we're told that "as far as the east is from the west, so far has he removed our transgressions from us"; and Paul wrote, "If anyone is in Christ, he is a new creation; the old has gone, the new has come" (2 Corinthians 5:17). No matter how much clutter we're dragging behind us, God lets us begin again. The trick to realizing that freedom is this: we have to let go of the junk. We do that by giving it to God.

It sounds simple enough, but it's amazing how hard it can be to do. Like those boxes of stuff we keep moving from house to house, all that junk from years of living stays with us because we've really become kind of attached to it. It's what defines us, or it has up until now. God longs to make us the people he designed us to be, and we want to cooperate, but we're not yet sure who that is. We're comfortable with the old person we've always been, even if we haven't been all that happy being that person.

If you're not sure where to start, how to begin, or where to put all the old stuff you're throwing out, I've got some encouraging news: once you've opened the door to Christ and invited him into your life, he helps you spot whatever it is you don't need anymore. And he's the paragon of graciousness. He'll show you where to start but never force you. Best of all, he even does the cleaning. But make no mistake—God will never be satisfied with just part of your life. He'll keep gently nudging until you give him your all.

When I first became a Christian, I was happy to have Jesus as part of my life—but I definitely compartmentalized my life and allowed him access only to certain parts. I didn't want him to mess with some parts of my life: my finances, my job, my relationships, my fun. Going to church was enough, wasn't it? Surely I didn't have to surrender everything! But the Holy Spirit wouldn't leave me alone. "Erik, what about over there?" I felt him say. I was ashamed of many of the areas he pointed out. I didn't want God looking at those parts of my life. It took about five years of spiritual struggle to realize that I had to surrender fully. All of it. Everything. No holding back. God wants it all. It's not that he's greedy—don't get me wrong. It's just that he knows how to handle it, and I had to admit that all I'd done up until then was make a mess of things.

How do we fully surrender our lives to God? First we need to recognize our true condition. The Bible can help us do that. As we read, it becomes a mirror that we hold up to ourselves to see our lives as God sees them. What's more, the Bible records the stories of men and women of faith whose lives—failures as well as successes—provide examples that teach us how to live our own lives to please God. Of course, the ultimate example of a life surrendered to God is Jesus. We can learn much from his teaching, his actions, his attitudes, and his relationship with God and with others. Here's what the author of Hebrews says: "Since we are surrounded by such a huge crowd of witnesses to the life of faith, let us strip off every weight that slows us down, especially the sin that so easily trips us up. And let us run with endurance the race God has set before us. We do this by keeping our eyes on Jesus, the champion who initiates and perfects our faith" (Hebrews 12:1–2 NLT). Keeping your eyes on Jesus—that's the key. Don't switch your focus to anything or anyone else! He is your champion.

I hope you'll discover, as I finally did, that there's no point in hiding the messes of your life from God—he already knows what they are. Let him into every room of your heart. Yes, you will experience some pain in the process; but I believe that if you recognize God's cleansing power for the positive force that it is, you'll learn to welcome it. After all, God is here to help you move into your new home. He just wants to make sure it's a home with him at the center.

Out with the Old and In with the New

Elizabeth had a "right" to the feelings that gripped her heart. Her second child had just been born when her husband left her for another woman.

As she prepared to take their son to visit Daddy and the "other woman" for the first time, she decided to bake some cookies. But her motives were far from loving. Her plan was to add, as the final ingredient, a big helping of spit. "I was overcome with wicked joy as I mixed the butter, sugar, eggs, and flour. I imagined watching them eat the cookies, secretly laughing to myself, as they took bite after bite."

Then God stopped her in her tracks. "It was like he tapped me on the shoulder and said, 'What are you doing?' I tried to ignore him. This was the only way I knew how to deal with the pain that felt like a constant knife stabbing my heart. I knew I was wrong, but I challenged him: 'Well, what else would you have me do?'

"Jesus reminded me that only he had a right to be vengeful and that he could handle the situation much better than I. My job was to forgive them. Overcome with shame, I fell on my knees and asked for forgiveness. Then I forgave my husband and his girlfriend. I finished up the cookies, spit-free, weeping as I scooped out each one and praying for God to enter into their hearts."

Since the day Elizabeth obeyed God and showed love to her ex-husband and his new wife, the Holy Spirit has been at the center of her life, directing her actions. She has become a significant member of a small group at her church, has traveled on two mission trips to Rwanda, and is actively ministering to others in need.

Like Elizabeth, you'll need to let God into every room, every closet, and even those dark places you don't talk about to anyone. In order for him to make you into the image of his Son, you've got to give every facet of your life into his caring hands.

I am certain that God,
who began the good work within you,
will continue his work until it is finally
finished on the day when Christ Jesus returns.
Philippians 1:6 NLT

God wants your new life to be ordered and intentional. You partner with him in this task by developing true intimacy with him through prayer and by holding nothing back. God wants your life to be marked by freedom and fulfillment, but he knows there's only one way for that to happen.

God's Liberating Presence

During her early twenties, Amy experienced devastating losses that, coupled with circumstances from her childhood, left her empty and despairing. "It felt like a tidal wave was threatening to take me out of the game completely," she said. "God finally had me in a place where I would listen, and I accepted Jesus Christ into my life. At long last, true freedom and fulfillment were within reach.

"God has patiently and graciously worked through the rubble, clearing a space for me to see who I really am. When you come to that place of freedom in Christ, you find fulfillment despite life's challenging circumstances. My soul is at rest, knowing God is going to use me, just the way I am, to further his plan and purpose for my life. The satisfaction is found in obeying him and in knowing he has planned this all along."

What undiscovered plans does God have for you? No matter how bad your life has been, you can find, as Amy did, that he is ready and willing to give you a brand-new beginning. In the book of Isaiah, we find a key signpost pointing to the Messiah who was to come: "I, the LORD, have called you in righteousness; I will take hold of your hand. I will keep you and will make you to be a covenant for the people and a light for the Gentiles, to open eyes that are blind, to free captives from prison and to release from the dungeon those who sit in darkness" (Isaiah 42:6–7). Amy, Elizabeth, and I have surrendered to this liberating Savior. Have you? Are you ready to make a fresh start today?

> God always comes first. He is always
> at the heart of life. He influences and invades
> all of reality. He *is*, and there is no other.
> Why does this make all the difference?
> Because then my happiness is not dependent
> on my personal experience, but on
> God's grace and love for me. Of course,
> this is the very heart of the gospel.
> —Josh Moody, *The God-Centered Life*

God longs for intimacy with you, and intimacy with him is a longing built inside each of us—even those who vigorously deny it. The way to establish that close relationship is through regular, daily conversations with him—beginning with a daily prayer of surrender. When you make this prayer a habit, you'll find that life in your new "house" is far less cluttered. Christ will help you keep the list short, regularly tossing what you don't need so that it doesn't pile up, and you will have discovered the key to living the surrendered life.

I hope you're getting the message Amy got: only you can be you, but if your life is cluttered with the junk you keep dragging around, the real you will be dramatically hindered. Tell God that you're ready for that new life through an initial act of surrender, a daily determination to remain yielded, and time spent daily in conversation with God. Then you'll find the real you shining through.

Making It Count

Over the past seven days, we've held up to examination in many areas of our lives to see if we're living in a truly surrendered way. Honestly, we've just covered what the apostle Paul said in Romans 12:1, to surrender our bodies—our entire bodies. That includes our minds, hearts, souls, and strength—everything. I've learned that these are the exact areas that so often get in the way of my becoming all God created me to be.

As I said, it was a while before I learned to surrender to God—and then to surrender daily. Since that point of surrender, I've been careful to include God in all my decisions. The result? My stress has been replaced with his peace.

Where do you want his peace? Where do you want his lordship? It has been said that Christ is either Lord of all or he's not Lord at all. If you still have areas in your life to surrender to him, don't let another second go by without doing so. Admit that you need him to be in charge of all of your life, not just certain parts. Invite him into every room. Ask Christ to set up headquarters in your heart. Make God the center of your life today.

Then, find a way to remind yourself every morning to surrender each day to him. I keep a baton next to my bed that I mentally hand to God each morning. The baton represents my life. I make it my goal to return each night knowing that God is still holding the baton. Before going to bed, I reflect back on my day and celebrate the times I didn't take the baton back.

The surrendered heart knows peace of mind, has power to live, and is driven by a purpose for living. By now you might be tired of lists, but I'm asking you to make one more. Naming what we're surrendering is a critical part of the process. So, one more time, write down what you have surrendered in the space below, and record today's date.

Date:

Now let's tell God we're ready to move.

Father, I thank you for helping me, over these past few days, to see all the things I've been hanging on to that really aren't getting me anywhere—except stuck in the same old place. You are stirring inside me a desire to follow you on a path that may be unknown to me at the moment, but I know you'll be with me. I offer up to you this list of all the things I want to surrender—the old life, the destructive sound tracks, the roles and relationships, the cravings, and those dreams I thought were just for me. Show me how to lay them down and not take them up again, but instead to walk a healthy, balanced, productive life—with my heart now beating wholly for you. I ask this in Jesus' name, amen.

When you look back at this page at some time in the future, you'll be able to see where you really did let go of what was holding you back—and you'll be able to see what God has done in your life as a result.

Tomorrow we'll talk about making Life Choice 2: Steward Your Unique Style Wisely. See you then!

LIFE CHOICE 2

*Steward Your
Unique Style Wisely*

LIFE ON LOAN

Use It or Lose It

We are God's masterpiece. He has created us anew
in Christ Jesus, so we can do the good things
he planned for us long ago.
Ephesians 2:10 NLT

Wise stewardship of your life
begins by understanding your shape.
—Rick Warren, The Purpose Driven Church

WHEN MOST OF US reach our teens, a mechanism switches on inside us that causes us to respond to parental advice with words something like these: "It's *my* life, and I can do what I want with it!" It must be connected to the same wire that causes us to turn up the stereo volume to earsplitting decibel levels. At any rate, this theme of personal ownership is one we frequently hear elsewhere on the world stage: *my* body, *my* time, *my* life. Where does this notion come from—that the life I did nothing to generate belongs exclusively to me? Is it really my life?

There's a song I've heard called "We Live on Borrowed Time." That's true, for our lives certainly don't belong to us. Life was God's idea. People are also God's idea. Everything we have comes from him. When we grasp this concept, it becomes clear to us that our job is to steward, or manage, those lives—and all the other things God has given us—for him. Once we've accepted Christ and have been guaranteed eternal life, why should God leave us here on earth for even one more second unless it's to serve him with the lives he has given us? God intends for us to make good use of his precious gift of life.

Life Choice 2, our focus for this week, is to steward your unique style wisely. We steward when we supervise an event or manage property on behalf of someone else. God has given all of us talents, a limited amount of time on earth, passions, money, experiences, relationships, and a purpose. It's all his, and only ours on loan for a brief time. He expects us to manage and make the most of these gifts for his glory.

Here's how the apostle Paul saw "his" life: "Christ Jesus made me his prisoner," Paul told the Ephesian church, "so that I could help you Gentiles" (Ephesians 3:1 CEV). Paul saw himself as serving Christ by reaching out to the people in Ephesus, who had not grown up in the Jewish traditions. To the Jew, any non-Jew is a Gentile. Paul continued: "You have surely heard about God's kindness in choosing me to help you" (Ephesians 3:2 CEV). Before his conversion, Paul had been one of the most zealous persecutors of Christ's followers. Paul was a willing participant in the martyrdom of Stephen (Acts 7:1–8:1) and readily admitted: "I persecuted the followers of this Way to their death, arresting both men and women and throwing them into prison" (Acts 22:4). So when God broke through to Paul's heart, his response was one of intense gratitude. He saw his role in founding churches as a privilege. In Ephesians 3:7–8 Paul declared, "God treated me with kindness. His power worked in me, and it became my job to spread the good news. I am the least important of all God's people. But God was kind and chose me to tell the Gentiles that because of Christ there are blessings that cannot be measured" (CEV).

Paul, who for years had passionately persecuted Christians, realized that his life had been spared for one purpose: to deliver with even greater zeal the good news of Christ to a lost and dying world. Pastor Tom Holladay has explained that Paul saw himself as a manager of God's mystery (Ephesians 3). To people without Christ, God's Word is a mystery. We can't possibly understand it until the Holy Spirit gives us understanding. God chose Paul as an early servant to help establish the church. Because of what God had shown him, Paul saw clearly what God wants all of us to understand, and he made it his mission from that day forward to take God's message to the world. His role was to oversee this mystery of God and to skillfully unwrap it for the sake of others.[1]

That same trust is ours today. We may or may not be called to start churches, plan crusades, or travel the globe as missionaries, but we all are assigned to be on a mission for Christ during our time on earth. Of all that God has given us to manage for him, this is undoubtedly Job One. We'll talk more about the specifics of our job description in week three, but for now it's important to realize that we each must ask ourselves daily, "How can I steward my unique gifts for Christ today? What can I do that will best serve God?"

Stewarding the Unique Style of You

"I quit!" Korede told her boss. After years of working at a job for which she was well educated and trained—but which she hated—she'd finally hit the wall. What else could she do?

Her journey of discovery took her into a multitude of part-time professions and a season that included reading both *The Purpose Driven Life,* by Rick Warren, and my book, *S.H.A.P.E.: Finding and Fulfilling Your Unique Purpose for Life.* "I realized God has created each one of us uniquely in order to serve him and fulfill our purpose," she told me. "From a young age I had enjoyed speaking to people, reading novels, and also writing. My favorite subjects in school had been within the arts. I had been doing these things all the while, but it had never occurred to me that they were the secret of my finding fulfillment. I only recollect that people used to tell me how much they loved reading what I had written or how much they enjoyed what I had spoken about.

"To the glory of God, I began to pay attention and the Lord began to open doors for me. Presently, I write regularly for three different magazines, have written about four books to date, teach Bible study in my church regularly, and conduct training seminars to help others discover their purpose. Each time I have an opportunity to speak to people or to write about something, I find I have energy and zeal. When I am feeling a little low, I just pick up my laptop and begin to write. My joy is instantly renewed."

Stewardship is the act of organizing
your life so that God can spend you.
—Lynn A. Miller

Korede was learning the difference between ownership (having abilities you think are yours to use or throw away) and stewardship (understanding that your abilities were given to you by God and are intended to bless others). Stewards understand that what they have is a trust, to be well cared for in the Master's absence. What does Christ expect you to do until he returns?

A key to discovering this answer is to look to God himself. Ask him to help you find out how he has uniquely made you. Take to heart what the Bible says about how much God loves you, in words like these: "The LORD your God is with you, he is mighty to save. He will take great delight in you, he will quiet you with his love, he will rejoice over you with singing" (Zephaniah 3:17).

God has designed you to make a specific difference in the time he has given you. You'll hear that theme a lot from me. Once you discover the amazing person God made you to be, you can begin to unravel the what, how, where, and when of your life. Nothing brings more satisfaction than discovering your unique mission.

What have you always loved to do? Are you realizing yet that God put that longing inside you? One college professor I interviewed recently said, "I just loved explaining things to people. So I figured out how to do that and get paid for it." If there's anything in your life that you just can't do in some way and at some time, consider that this natural enthusiasm is God-given. Ask him to show you how to steward your passion in ways that maximize the benefits for his sake.

In Ephesians 2:10 God calls us his workmanship, or, in the original language, *poema*. Think of it: you are God's poem!

Only you can be you, which means only you can do what God made you uniquely to do. What unique aspects of you is God asking you to steward for him? How does he want you to manage your life on loan—your passions, your finances, your life experiences, your relationships, and your career? These are the questions we'll be exploring in greater depth this week.

Making It Count

To him who is able to do immeasurably more than all we ask or imagine, according to his power that is at work within us, to him be glory in the church and in Christ Jesus throughout all generations, for ever and ever! Amen.

—Ephesians 3:20–21

These days we hear a lot about taking care of our planet. It has become a hot-button issue, dividing those who believe we are in a global warming crisis from those who believe we are simply experiencing a cycle of nature. I'm not here to take sides, but the passion involved with this argument shows that people the world over, no matter where they fall on the question of faith, understand the concept of stewardship. We have a responsibility to take care of what God has given us, from our natural resources to our possessions to our personal attributes.

Whether you have fully discovered the unique work God has for you to do is not as critical as the fact that you relentlessly pursue it. The joy is in the continual discovery. As you look into how God wants to use each of the unique aspects of the life he has built inside you, I hope you feel your heart pound with the possibilities. For if there is one thing you can be certain of, it is that as long as you draw breath, his work in you is not finished. He will continue to perfect that work until Christ comes again (Philippians 1:6). The possibilities for what God wants to do in and through your life are more than you can imagine.

Today, reflect on the fact that your life truly is on loan from God, yours to use or to lose. Think about our discussion of your uniqueness. Ponder the truth of Ephesians 2:10 in several Bible translations to receive all the richness of its meaning.

- "We are God's workmanship, created in Christ Jesus to do good works, which God prepared in advance for us to do" (NIV).
- "We are God's masterpiece. He has created us anew in Christ Jesus, so we can do the good things he planned for us long ago" (NLT).
- "God has made us what we are. In Christ Jesus, God made us to do good works, which God planned in advance for us to live our lives doing" (NCV).
- "We are God's [own] handiwork (His workmanship), recreated in Christ Jesus, [born anew] that we may do those good works which God predestined (planned beforehand) for us [taking paths that he prepared ahead of time], that we should walk in them [living the good life that he prearranged and made ready for us to live]" (Amplified).
- "He creates each of us by Christ Jesus to join him in the work he does, the good work he has gotten ready for us to do, work we had better be doing" (MSG).

Those last few words say so much: the stewardship of our uniqueness in Christ is "work we had better be doing." Don't miss out on it!

Write in the space below your thoughts on Ephesians 2:10. Since only you can be you, how do you intend to use this life that is yours on loan from God? In what ways do you plan to participate in the work God is doing in your generation? Your life is a gift from God. What you do with it is your gift back to him.

My Thoughts on Ephesians 2:10

Here's one more verse to ponder today, from the Message: "If you grasp and cling to life on your terms, you'll lose it, but if you let that life go, you'll get life on God's terms" (Luke 17:33 MSG). What does it mean to you to find life on God's terms? What are you willing to let go of to get it?

We'll spend the rest of the week unpacking this idea of stewardship. I think you'll agree that God has an exciting plan for each of us, through life lived to the fullest in every way possible. Tomorrow's discussion focuses on your amazing talents.

Here's a prayer to help you get going:

Father, remind us that we are your unique creations. With surrendered hearts, we ask you to open our eyes to the work you desire to do through our lives—the work you have already prepared for us to do. Help us to live each day wisely with eternity in mind, seeing ourselves as stewards of what you have entrusted to us. We ask this in your Son's name . . . Amen!

TREASURE CHEST

Uncovering Your True Talents

God has given us different gifts for doing certain things well.
Romans 12:6 NLT

When I stand before God at the end of my life,
I would hope that I would not have a single bit of talent left,
and could say, "I used everything you gave me."
—Erma Bombeck

AVE YOU EVER GONE on a treasure hunt? Imagine that you're a member of Captain Jack's rogues' gallery and you've just come upon a map to treasures untold. You study it, figure out your compass headings, pack up for a year's journey, and prepare to set sail. When you finally come upon the treasure, the bountiful booty is stored in an ornate, brass-bound chest that can be unlocked only with an enormous filigreed key.

That's a story worthy of the movies. But it's not how God works. Did you know that God has chosen to bury his unequaled treasure in ordinary clay pots? Would you believe that you are one of those clay pots? That's what Scripture tells us: "We now have this light shining in our hearts, but we ourselves are like fragile clay jars containing this great treasure. This makes it clear that our great power is from God, not from ourselves" (2 Corinthians 4:7 NLT).

God has entrusted his greatest treasure—his message of hope—to us. To help unearth it on behalf of others, he has given each of us certain abilities. Do you know what special treasures God has buried within you? Finding this buried treasure is imperative. God does not mean for it to remain hidden.

Your Buried Treasure Map

What are you good at? I'm not talking about *American Idol* good, although you might be that amazing. But what do you do well? About what do you hear others say, "I love that thing you do"?

When she was ten years old, my daughter Shaya wanted to try out for some activities. All the kids in the cul-de-sac were playing soccer, so she tried it for a while. She wasn't enjoying herself, but I kept pushing her: "You can do this!" I grew up playing team sports, so the competitive spirit came naturally to me.

Then came the game I remember like it was yesterday. Shaya was playing defense. But instead of going after the ball, she was looking for flowers. It was like a scene from a *Peanuts* cartoon. Difficult as it was, we faced the fact that maybe God hadn't wired her for soccer. Today Shaya's swimming trophies line our mantel. What Shaya needed most was for her dad to get out of the way and admit that God had made her unique.

You, too, are a unique creation of God. There never has been and never will be another you. What have you been wired to do? Have you found it, or are you still picking flowers on the soccer field, hoping the ball doesn't mash your bouquet? The good news is that God has also programmed you with markers to help you determine whether you're doing what he made you to do.

Stress is one of those markers. When you feel unduly stressed by a particular activity, it may be a clue that you're doing something outside your design. What is your stress level like these days? Do you love going to work, dread Mondays, or think, *It's just a job: it'll do until something better comes along?*

When we discover who we are and commit ourselves to living for God's glory, God's kingdom, and God's work, our success and satisfaction levels go up, our self-worth and self-image are elevated, we feel significant . . . and our stress levels take a dive. What could be simpler to figure out?

This is not to say that when we're doing what God intends us to do, we'll never feel stressed. Of course we will. Stress is part of life. But when you're doing what you're meant to do, the stress feels less like frustration and more like part of the game. Think of it as the difference between the stress you feel when you're stuck in traffic on your way to work at a job you really don't like and the deadline pressure you feel as you work to complete a project that is a labor of love.

God really doesn't make life as hard as we think it is. As one friend recently told me, "When I operate in the area of my giftedness, I feel complete joy." That's not a bad return on investment for just being you. Learn to recognize the stress markers in your life. Like your own treasure map or personal GPS, those markers will help keep you on the road to discovering God's perfect plan for you and will confirm the discovery of God's hidden bounty in your life.

Comparison Shopping

Here's a huge problem I've observed after meeting with thousands of people: we don't accept ourselves as God made us. "I wish I were different! God messed up when he made me. I should be different." Whether it's taller, shorter, wider, thinner, more hair, less hair, or whatever, it seems we're all dissatisfied with something about ourselves. As if we needed the help, the media is telling us all day long: "You can be anything you want to be." It's not true. You can only be what you were made to be—and that's you! So rather than stress over what you can't do or be, discover what you love most and then find a way to use it for God's kingdom.

The Bible, often referred to as God's love letter to his church, tells us we are God's works of art. That's how much God values us! If the God of the universe, the Master Designer, values us so highly, why waste time comparing ourselves with others and dishonoring God by trying to be something or someone we're not?

Oh, don't worry; we wouldn't dare say
that we are as wonderful as these other men
who tell you how important they are!
But they are only comparing themselves
with each other, using themselves as the
standard of measurement. How ignorant!
2 Corinthians 10:12 NLT

God made each of us to accomplish a specific mission in life. He wants each of us to play our part. Now, don't get me wrong . . . God's plan will still prevail even if you don't get this message. But you will have missed out on your reason for living. I know you don't want that to happen.

In Galatians 6:4 the apostle Paul gave us a road map for getting it right: "Make a careful exploration of who you are and the work you have been given [your purpose], and then sink yourself into that" (MSG). Paul is essentially saying, "You only get one life, so put everything you can into living it." In the middle of this advice, Paul presses the Pause button to interject, "Don't be impressed with yourself. Don't compare yourself with others" (Galatians 6:5 MSG). He recognized the traps and snares that so easily entangle us. We can be distracted, either by thinking we're hot stuff or by wishing we were like someone else.

When we become overly impressed with ourselves, we are in danger of abusing God's grace. It's what got Satan and his gang tossed out of heaven. The book of Isaiah tells us about the devil's great ego. Once

Satan became so stuck on himself, he actually thought he was greater than God: "You said in your heart, 'I will ascend to heaven; I will raise my throne above the stars of God; I will sit enthroned on the mount of assembly, on the utmost heights of the sacred mountain. I will ascend above the tops of the clouds; I will make myself like the Most High'" (Isaiah 14:13–14). But, as Satan learned, no one is greater than God Almighty. God, in his righteousness, cast Satan and all his followers from heaven: "You are brought down to the grave, to the depths of the pit" (Isaiah 14:15). Such are the perils of thinking too highly of ourselves.

By the same token, when we waste time wishing we could sing like Mariah Carey, look like Brad Pitt, or preach like Billy Graham, we are dishonoring God's wisdom in creating us. Instead, we should ask God to show us how he wants to be glorified through us. When we behave as if God somehow made a mistake in creating us, we are guilty of turning things upside down: rather than gratefully acknowledging that God as Creator made us in a way that pleased him, we think he's like us—fallible—and that he couldn't possibly have meant to make us this way. Isaiah had it right when he said, "How foolish can you be? He is the Potter, and he is certainly greater than you, the clay! Should the created thing say of the one who made it, 'He didn't make me'? Does a jar ever say, 'The potter who made me is stupid'?" (Isaiah 29:16 NLT).

Best-selling author Cecil Murphey admits that this lesson is not an easy one to learn. Here's how he sees the dangers of "comparison shopping":

> When we compare ourselves to others, we experience negative feelings, and in my case, years ago jealousy. Other emotions arise such as insecurity and a sense of unworthiness. We focus on what we're not instead of who we are. As long as we feel the need to compare, we can't win. We'll constantly see someone who is more talented, achieves more, gets better breaks, or is better qualified. (Some people compare themselves and feel superior, but that's not my experience.) A few years ago I decided not to focus on others' achievements but on my own. I can be only me,

and my task is to be the best Cec Murphey I can. Some people are more gifted than I am; some are less gifted. My responsibility is to be faithful to who I am and what I can do. I thought of the words of Jesus to Peter. In the final chapter of John's Gospel, Jesus tells Peter how he will die. Instead of focusing on himself, Peter points to John and asks, "What about him?" "What is that to you? You must follow me," Jesus says (John 21:22). Here's the practical thing I've done. I pray for those of whom I'm tempted to feel jealous. I ask God to bless them as richly as possible. Their success has no bearing on my achievements. The more I champion others, the less I need to compare and the greater my level of inner peace.[1]

The apostle Paul, it seems, would agree: "Each of you must take responsibility for doing the creative best you can with your own life" (Galatians 6:5 MSG). When Christ is your measuring stick, God's grace will always be sufficient to help you gauge your growth.

If you'd gone on a real-life treasure hunt and actually found buried treasure, would you complain that it wasn't the right stuff? I don't think so. Thank God for what he has given you, and seek to steward it responsibly for his sake.

Becoming God's Unburied Treasure

"Don't waste time with college," the high school counselor told Debbie. "You won't make it." Determined not to let anyone think she was stupid, Debbie responded by throwing herself into her work. "By sixteen I was running an ice-cream store by myself," she told me. "I did go to college, and then I became a workaholic."

Debbie took a job in a clothing store at the mall, a likely place to meet professional women. And meet them she did, including the wife of a bank president, who gave her a chance at the career she longed for by arranging an interview for Debbie at her husband's bank. Before long, Debbie was climbing the corporate ladder. In the middle of this rocket ride, she and her husband rededicated their lives to Christ and began seeking his direction for their lives. It took a while, but eventually she let go of the job and allowed God to redirect her dreams.

"I got involved in women's ministry by volunteering at my church. I helped lead a women's Bible study, so my leadership skills were being used, but now totally out of a servant's heart."

Today Debbie plays a leadership role in women's ministry at her church. "God had a role in mind that involved serving his people. He created me before I was born, just as he created every other woman or man. And now I get the privilege . . . to do what I was designed to do."

Sooner or later, all of us will stand before our maker to answer a few questions. The first and most critical is this: "What did you do with my Son, Jesus? Did you receive him or did you reject him?" Then he will ask, "What did you do with what I gave you?" What are you going to say to that?

Paul said in 1 Corinthians 15:10, "By the grace of God I am what I am." Be grateful for who and what you are, because you are what God made you to be. Give yourself permission to understand who you are so that you can make the difference God designed you to make. Become his unburied treasure to enrich the lives of others.

First Who, Then What

In the book *Good to Great,* author Jim Collins examines the success tactics of companies that made the leap from being average to being market leaders. He explains that in every case, the companies first identified their key personnel—before they'd even decided what their business was about. Collins calls it the "first who, then what" principle.[2]

I've observed that many of us get the process of discovering our purpose backward. We ask, "What should I do with my life?" when our first question should be, "Who am I?" As a result, we end up frustrated and fatigued—certainly not fulfilled.

Who you are always indicates what God wants you to do with your life. A good place to begin answering that first question is by discovering your strengths. It's not about what you think you should be able to do well; it's about what you actually do well.

In his article "The Law of Differences: Life or Death for Relationships," Dr. Michael Sanders explains that simple observation tells us that none of us possesses every human strength. It stands to reason that an aggressive problem solver might lack the careful consideration of someone with a more reflective nature. But both qualities are desirable.[3] As a group, we wouldn't want to be without either of those strengths. So just because you don't paint or write as well as your friend doesn't mean your ability to coach a Little League softball team is any less important or needed.

Our world needs people with all strengths so that we might effectively solve a host of problems. When we work together in community, each of us puts his or her strengths to work on behalf of others. All too often, though, we work in opposition to one another. It's easy to complain, "We just don't have anything in common." But God didn't make us to be alike! What a boring world it would be if he had. Instead, we should celebrate our differences and thank God for making us with unique abilities to use in building his kingdom.

Since we find ourselves fashioned into all
these excellently formed and marvelously
functioning parts in Christ's body,
let's just go ahead and be what we were
made to be, without enviously or pridefully
comparing ourselves with each other,
or trying to be something we aren't.
Romans 12:6 MSG

It's tragic how many of us have lost our concept of what we love to do. Just to get by, we get stuck in a rut of doing what we need to do or what we think we should do. The stress and pressure weigh us down, but we don't know how to escape it. If that describes you, the way out is to rediscover your dreams. Find a way to use those things God has predisposed you to love. Let him liberate you to be the person he made you to be and to fully play the role he has created especially for you.

Making It Count

One way to help yourself decide what your true strengths are is to make a list of the abilities you use on a regular basis and rate each one. Using a 1 to 3 numbering system, determine which of these things rock your world (1), which are satisfying (2), and which you do but could live without (3). For me, coaching, consulting, and communicating are all 1's; strategic planning and problem solving are 2. Dealing with details and deadlines I could live without. Please use the list of abilities on page 239 to help you with this exercise.

Things I Do on a Regular Basis   **Rating (1-2-3)**

Once you've got your list, ask someone you trust and who knows you well to look over it with you. Invite this person to speak honestly regarding those areas he or she believes you would do well to pursue. Then offer that list to God with open hands, and ask him to show you how to use those abilities for his kingdom's sake. If you're already using your natural skills for God, may he bless you richly in all you do for him.

As we part company today, I urge you to take time to read the parable of the talents, recorded both in Matthew 25:14–30 and in Luke 19:12–27. Reflect on the servants who were faithful with what the Master had given them as opposed to the one who was afraid and hid his talent. Whom do you want to be like?

According to some surveys, 87 percent of people in America are unhappy in their jobs.[4] If that includes you, consider how you can surrender your attitude to God as you wait for a new position that better uses your treasure chest of abilities. Begin to outline a plan for making the most of what's in your treasure chest.

If your current profession is not releasing the treasures inside of you, please use my "Developing a 5 Star Career" tools online at www.onlyyoucanbeyou.com.

Let's pray together.

Father, we ask you to give us eyes to see the unique treasures you've buried inside each of us and to inspire us with ideas for how to use that treasure in your service. We want to live to please you and not to waste the time with which you've blessed us. Help us to desire to be all you've designed us to be, and then to live our lives to the fullest. Help us as we seek to wisely steward the abilities you've given us for your glory. We ask this in Jesus' name . . . Amen.

Spiritual gifts are not the same as natural abilities, but God wants to use both in our lives, often in conjunction with each other. We'll open that treasure chest tomorrow. See you back at the coffee bar!

Day 10

FOR YOU

Embracing Your Spiritual Gifts

This salvation, which was first announced by the Lord,
was confirmed to us by those who heard him. God also testified
to it by signs, wonders and various miracles, and gifts of the
Holy Spirit distributed according to his will.
Hebrews 2:3–4

Now about the gifts of the Spirit, brothers and sisters,
I do not want you to be uninformed.
1 Corinthians 12:1 TNIV

God has given us all a sweet spot—in fact, Paul says that
God has given us the gift of a sweet spot so that we could
serve God and produce the maximum result and maximum
satisfaction both for God and for us.
—Bruce Emmert

Y ou've just moved into your new home, and now a friend comes
by with a housewarming gift. "For you!" he says. "Thank you. May
I open it?" you reply. And naturally, that is what any of us would do. So
why is it that so many of us haven't opened the spiritual gifts that God
has given us? In fact, many are unaware that God has given us spiritual

gifts at all. How can we serve in his kingdom if we don't know what he's given us to serve him with?

Penny had a group of women meeting weekly in her home to study the Bible. As in most groups, some were new believers and others had been Christians for years. But when they began to examine the gifts of the Holy Spirit, only one or two were aware of their spiritual gifts. "I've known what my spiritual gifts were for many years but just didn't know what to do with that knowledge," Penny admitted. Now, at the age of sixty-seven, she thought she might be too old to be of much use. As a result of her group's study, Penny now sees that she is a uniquely created human being with much to offer her community.

"I listened to the Lord, and I'm now taking a correspondence course in biblical counseling. I'm loving it and learning so much. I know that God is leading me step by step toward my dream to counsel women. My desire is to learn and grow in the Lord and help other women to do the same."

All the women in Penny's group are discovering their unique abilities to serve the Lord. One volunteers at a blood bank, another tutors at local schools, and another serves at a local mission. "It has been a joy to watch them use their gifts in our community," Penny said. These women are living proof that it is never too late to serve God by using what he has given you.

We can be intimidated by the topic of spiritual gifts because it seems so mysterious. But when we "unwrap" them by taking time to discover what God has given us, we learn that they're not mysterious at all but readily available and waiting to be used. We simply need to be informed about them, as Paul said in his first letter to the church at Corinth.

Understanding Spiritual Gifts

Spiritual gifts are not the same as natural abilities. While both are given to us by God, they serve different purposes. Our abilities are inborn to help us get things done. But spiritual gifts are given to express God's love and strengthen his church. Abilities are given at birth. Spiritual gifts are endowed at rebirth—when we accept Christ into our lives. The apostle Peter explained: "Each of you has been blessed with one of God's many wonderful gifts to be used in the service of others. So use your gift well" (1 Peter 4:10 CEV).

Because we are uniquely made, it's critical to understand the nature of our spiritual gifts as well as God's intent for them. They are not given for our personal benefit but for us to use in service to others. The power to use them comes expressly from the Holy Spirit, who lives in you once you become a believer. God has a plan for how those gifts are to be used, so it's critical that you plug in to this power source for them to be effective.

Spiritual gifts are like abilities in that we must know what gifts we have been given in order to use them properly. Like the person who has the wrong job, those who serve in areas where they are not gifted end up frustrated. Our spiritual gifts may also propel us into careers that will utilize those gifts.

Karen has a heart for helping others. "My own teenage pregnancy gave me a passion for helping young girls either avoid or get through similar situations," she said. Life as a young mother of three girls kept Karen from attending college and continues to challenge her time management, but she is pursuing a path that allows her to use her spiritual gift of helping—combined with her past experience—in ways that build lives. She feels certain it's God-directed. "I'm not sure where God will lead me, but my heart burns bright to bring these girls hope, wisdom, and direction. I want my legacy to be changing and empowering the legacy of others." With the power of the Holy Spirit at work in her, Karen is using her life experience to bring change and hope to others.

Sandy has always loved children. Childless in her first marriage, she wondered if God would ever bring little ones into her life. When she first heard about spiritual gifts, she realized that God had already put her right where he wanted her, working with the children's-ministry programs at her church. "How thrilling to realize I was serving in my sweet spot. Children are my purpose. I love using my gift of teaching to help them learn about God. The true love of the Father has never flowed through me quite like this."

Opening Your Gifts

Are you getting the picture? When we serve God through the gifts he has given us, his Spirit does the work, we get the joy, and the body of Christ is strengthened. The beauty of it is that these gifts fit together with how God has created us uniquely to accomplish the specific purpose he made each of us to fulfill. How do you think God has gifted you? Write your thoughts in the space below.

Scripture uses five main passages to help us learn about spiritual gifts:

1. "In his grace, God has given us different gifts for doing certain things well. So if God has given you the ability to prophesy, speak out with as much faith as God has given you. If your gift is serving others, serve them well. If you are a teacher, teach well. If your gift is to encourage others, be encouraging. If it is giving, give generously. If God has given you leadership ability, take the responsibility seriously. And if you have a gift for showing kindness to others, do it gladly" (Romans 12:6–8 NLT).

2. "To one person the Spirit gives the ability to give wise advice; to another the same Spirit gives a message of special

knowledge. The same Spirit gives great faith to another, and to someone else the one Spirit gives the gift of healing. He gives one person the power to perform miracles, and another the ability to prophesy. He gives someone else the ability to discern whether a message is from the Spirit of God or from another spirit. Still another person is given the ability to speak in unknown languages, while another is given the ability to interpret what is being said" (1 Corinthians 12:8–10 NLT).

3. "In the church God has given a place first to apostles, second to prophets, and third to teachers. Then God has given a place to those who do miracles, those who have gifts of healing, those who can help others, those who are able to govern, and those who can speak in different languages" (1 Corinthians 12:28 NCV).

4. "These are the gifts Christ gave to the church: the apostles, the prophets, the evangelists, and the pastors and teachers" (Ephesians 4:11 NLT).

5. "Open your homes to each other, without complaining. Each of you has received a gift to use to serve others. Be good servants of God's various gifts of grace" (1 Peter 4:9–10 NCV).

From these passages, we can glean a list of twenty spiritual gifts. Based on what God has been speaking to your heart through his Word, see if you can identify one or more gifts that he wants you to use for him. For help understanding what these gifts are and how they function, turn to the section called "What's in Your Box?" on page 237.

Administration	Healing	Miracles
Apostleship	Helping	Pastoring
Discernment	Hospitality	Prophecy
Encouragement	Interpretation	Teaching

Evangelism	Knowledge	Speaking in tongues
Faith	Leadership	Wisdom
Giving	Showing mercy	

Write in the space below what you think God might want you to do with the gift(s) he has given you. Then commit your gifts to him in prayer. Keep in mind that one of the best ways to use your gifts to bless God's family (the reason he gave them to you) is by becoming an active member of a local church. You need to be in community with other growing believers.

My gifts   **Ways to use them**

If you're not sure about your gifts even after looking over this list, consider "trying on" different roles by volunteering in ministries at your church. I've seen it happen time and again: the people who serve are the most fulfilled members of our church. They seem to know why God made them and what he made them to do.

Though she may not have known where they came from at first, Rachel had no trouble discerning her spiritual gifts. As a child she would line up her dolls and stuffed animals and "preach" to them on a regular basis. Teaching came naturally to her, and today she teaches people wherever she can. God is using her in mighty ways to reach and strengthen the body of Christ as well as to bring her a joyful sense of fulfillment.

For others, the gifts God desires them to use to minister are not quite so obvious. Bob had taught in classrooms for years but never considered that God might want him to teach other believers. One day, when his pastor was not able to teach the final session of a class, he asked Bob to take it. "That final class went well, and through it I saw in a new way how God had uniquely made me. Several weeks later the door opened for me to begin serving as our church prayer coordinator, which has required the exercise of my administrative gifts and experience. That role has given me the opportunity to teach two adult Sunday-school classes on prayer as well as lead a prayer team. For the first time in many, many years, I believe I am fulfilling God's purpose for me in the church."

The Gift Thief

As a kid, did you ever feel tempted to take a birthday gift you really liked from someone else, or did you have one taken from you? We need to be aware that our enemy, Satan, is jealous of what God gives us, and he'll continually try to keep us from using our gifts effectively. Below are some common tactics the gift thief uses to steal our joy as well as our will and ability to use the gifts God has given to us.

Tactic 1. Making Someone Else's Gift Seem Better

Why do gifts and abilities always look bigger and better when someone else has them? Perhaps it's because we're not close enough to see them as they really are. As with our abilities, we're often tempted to compare our gifts with those of others. The bigger and brighter and shinier the gift, the more we may wish it were ours. Keep in mind that God has given us the gifts he desires us to have for his purposes. Remember, too, that it's not about serving ourselves but serving others. We can only be ourselves, so if we try to serve in ways in which we were not created to serve, we will only feel frustrated and empty. God does not make mistakes. Even if we're never on a stage or in the spotlight, God has the perfect place for us to shine.

Tactic 2. Fooling Us into Thinking Others Should Be Like Us

Whatever we do, we must not get caught in the trap of expecting others to be just like us. As I shared earlier, I've always been competitive in sports, so I naturally expected my kids to be the same way. That expectation led to frustration, both on my part and for my poor kids, until I finally got with the program and accepted the fact that they are uniquely created beings, formed for serving God in ways I could never imagine. It's critical for us to learn to love others as God made them, without expecting them to be like us.

Tactic 3. Tricking Us into Refusing God's Gifts

Satan also trips us up by causing us to refuse the gifts God has given us. Nothing makes me sadder than to see people miss their giftedness simply because they don't have a job or position that employs those gifts. Feelings of inadequacy are huge gift thieves. Don't let them deter you! If you long to serve Christ in a particular way, look for ways in which to do so. Whether it's leading a Bible study in your home, taking meals to shut-ins, or being a member of a care team, give yourself permission to be all God made you to be.

Tactic 4. Misleading Us about Our Gifts

Another favorite ruse of our enemy is fraud. He loves to make us think we have gifts we don't actually have. This lie distracts us from using the gifts we *do* have by keeping us in pursuit of what we *don't* have. This is perhaps most obvious when it comes to leadership. If you've been going down a road that is not being blessed, consider that you might be on the wrong path. Sincerely ask God to show you where he wants you to be. Facing this question will undoubtedly require courage on your part, because it'll require you to let go of that security blanket you've likely grasped for a long time. But when you release that hold and allow God to lead you into the areas he's always longed for you to travel, you'll find a sense of freedom and fulfillment you didn't know was possible.

The way to outsmart the gift thief is to focus on God, not the gifts. As wonderful as God's gifts are, they're not the ultimate goal. Rather, they are a means by which God allows us to partner with him to build his everlasting kingdom. Let him show you what he has given you, and then ask him to work through you to use those gifts for his glory.

The more you minister to others, the more clearly you'll see your gifts. The best news is that no set maturity level is required to have and use your gifts for God. In fact, there are no qualifications for being used by God. As long as you are a believer, God's Spirit is in you, and he's ready to empower you for his service.

Making It Count

You may be thinking that if you can just discover your gift, you'll know where you are supposed to serve in the body of Christ. But, as we discussed earlier, the key to discovering your gift(s) is most often found *through* serving in ministry. Now that you've identified a few possibilities, don't be afraid to go out and try on a few ministries for size. If you're already serving, ask yourself if what you're doing lines up with the gifts you believe God has revealed to you today. Don't be afraid to try something new to discover just where it is God wants you to shine.

Most birthday gifts wear out after a while and need to be replaced, or they run down and need recharging—like my son J.T.'s remote-control trucks. I should own stock in the battery company! But spiritual gifts are different. While they never weaken or need to be replaced, they can be reinforced and developed. You can attend seminars, take classes, or explore other options for learning new techniques. Whatever your gift or gifts are, find ways to improve them to become the best you possible.

When we're serving God with the spiritual gifts he has given us, we find freedom and fulfillment. Only you can be you, and there's no better way to express that than through your spiritual gifts. When you put them to work as God intended, you'll be strengthening the body of Christ and blessing the heart of God.

One other thing before we move on: when we serve, it's critical that we do so in an attitude of love. God is love (1 John 4:8), after all, and our primary role is to reflect God to a world desperate to know him. As you read Paul's messages in Scripture about God's gifts, notice that he always follows them with a few choice words about God's love. The gifts God has for us have been given for the express purpose of showing his love to a world desperately needing it. We are called to be God's hands and feet in this world.

Above all, our chief desire should be to serve God in any way he asks. We already know, based on our discussions so far, that he will not ask us to operate outside the unique way in which he made us. That said, whether he asks us to serve in ways great or small, we must be ready at all times to follow his command. He is our great and mighty God, and he will never require more of us than what he knows we can accomplish—when we rely on him to help.

Today, reflect on this advice from Paul to Timothy: "I remember your genuine faith. . . . And I know that same faith continues strong in you. This is why I remind you to fan into flames the spiritual gift God gave you when I laid my hands on you. For God has not given us a spirit of fear and timidity, but of power, love, and self-discipline. So never be ashamed to tell others about our Lord" (2 Timothy 1:5–8 NLT).

Can you feel those embers catching fire in your soul? This is what God asks of you and me, that we put to good use the gifts he freely gave us. Don't miss out on being who God made you to be.

Let's take a moment to pray together.

Father, thank you for the gifts you've given us for serving in the body of Christ. Give us a Christmas-morning enthusiasm for opening your gifts and for putting them to use to build your kingdom. Forgive us for neglecting them or underusing them before now. Our chief desire is to please you, Lord. In the name of Jesus, we ask you to show us how. Amen.

Think again about that image of flames. What is it that sets your heart on fire? Where do you want to make a difference in this world? Let's meet back here tomorrow and talk it over.

Day 11

JESUS CALLING

Finding Your Inner Passion

A great leader's courage to fulfill his vision
comes from passion, not position.
—John C. Maxwell

It isn't what you do, but how you do it.
—John Wooden

FOUR-YEAR-OLD DAVID LISTENED IN fascination to the sound coming from the stethoscope the pediatric ward nurse had put into his ears. "What do you suppose that is?" the nurse asked as she held the stethoscope's chest piece over his heart. David knitted his brows together and thought it over, then broke into a contagious grin as he figured it out. "Is that Jesus knocking?" he asked.

Have you ever heard Jesus knocking at the door of your heart? You may be familiar with the scripture that says, "Here I am! I stand at the door and knock. If you hear my voice and open the door, I will come in and eat with you, and you will eat with me" (Revelation 3:20 NCV). We often refer to this experience in terms of opening our hearts to Christ as our Savior, but I believe Jesus means for us to keep on listening for that knock even after we've invited him into our hearts.

When you're trying to figure out what your Christian calling might be, think of it as Jesus knocking, or ringing the doorbell of your heart. Whenever you hear it, it's most likely connected in some way to the unique plan God has for your life.

Your heart has been programmed to recognize certain activities as those you love to do. They come so naturally to you that you couldn't imagine living without them. They're more than just things you like to do, or even love to do. I'm talking about those activities, those passions, that drive your life.

Kay Warren has always had a heart for helping others, but one day she heard God knocking in a way that surprised her. She'd been reading a magazine article about children orphaned by AIDS in Africa. Normally, she would have skipped past it. After all, what could one American woman do to help those children? But something drew her eyes to these words: "twelve million children orphaned due to AIDS in Africa." That number disturbed her. She couldn't get past it. So she began talking with her husband about this pandemic and its devastating effects. Kay's obedient response to God's knock led her to take action that has already impacted thousands of lives.

Where do you hear Jesus knocking? Are you an achiever, someone who thrives on a sense of accomplishment? A dreamer who's always scaling impossible heights in your mind? Or are you a leader who takes charge and paves the way for others? When you hear that knock on the door of your heart, what does it make you want to do? Are you ready to answer the call—or would you rather pretend you're not home? If you haven't heard it yet, listen intently for God's knock. Then, when you hear it, answer the door. You'll never regret it.

Boldly Going

We live in a society that is known for enjoying comfort. Yet America was built by risk takers, people who believed in their dreams and followed them no matter the cost. When we speak of the American spirit, we refer to people like those pioneers who moved boldly forward into an unknown, uncharted world. Today, however, we're used to getting what we want when we want it. We don't even have to get out of our cars to get it. We like fast food, instant downloads, and constant noise. In fact, there's so much noise all around us, 24/7, that Jesus could be hammering away at our hearts and we might not be able to hear him.

Answering his knock on the door of your heart is going to require you to take a risk or two. There's no way around it, really. You may not have to learn to fly an airplane or go to China as a missionary or sell all your possessions, but you do have to ask yourself some hard questions, such as: How much do I really love God? What does God want me to do about this need I see? Am I willing to do *anything* he asks of me?

On the other hand, if you believe you hear Jesus knocking, what is it that's holding you back from answering? Consider the fact that God himself has placed certain desires in your heart. And he has promised to be with you every step of the way when you open the door to his calling. With a guarantee like that, what is there to be afraid of? You already said yes to God last week . . . remember? This is just the next step of that "yes."

Becky made a choice that many people would find questionable, at best, when she and her husband opened their home to a woman suffering from a lifetime of addiction and abuse. But for Becky it was the natural extension of her lifelong desire to help others, make them feel welcome, and help them find their direction in life. Once she realized those passions, she surrendered them to the Lord. Now, with an obedient heart, not only is she providing this woman and her son a home to live in, but Becky also has nurtured a relationship that allows her to guide this woman into making new and better choices for her life and for her son's future. "Each day I have the privilege of shepherding her by discussing her fears and problems," Becky said. "We are working together to help her tackle each one with Christ's help. I am absolutely in my element."

Work willingly at whatever you do, as though you were working for the Lord rather than for people. Remember that the Lord will give you an inheritance as your reward, and that the Master you are serving is Christ.

Colossians 3:23–24 NLT

Whether it's writing symphonies, feeding the poor, working with children, or solving global crises, God has put a stirring in your heart to make a difference with your life. Surrendering your dream to him does not mean forgetting about it. Rather, it means pursuing it with all your heart and leaving the results to God.

Naming your passion is the next step in becoming the unique you that God created you to be. The seed of that passion was planted in you at birth. He's just been waiting for you to discover it.

Passion Drivers

When you examine the lives of people who achieved great things for God, you'll find several things that show up again and again. These common factors are the drivers that kept them going. We can use these as pointers and apply them to our own lives by asking ourselves some questions.

- What is it that's propelling me forward?
- Who or what grabs my heart?
- What person or group of people would I love to help?

- How can I help them? (Determine which needs these people have that you intend to meet.)
- What principle or cause will I take on? (Identify the problem you intend to help solve.)
- What is it that I need to accomplish before it's too late? (Discover what it is that God has called you to do for his kingdom's sake.)

Some of us feel passion-driven all our lives—compelled to accomplish a particular mission—while others struggle to identify what that something is. As with discovering our spiritual gifts, we might have to jump in and try a few things before we see what lights that fire inside us.

Motivational speaker and sports professional Pat Williams says passion comes from loving what you do and welcoming the competition. He explains: "It's the competition that drags out of us that which we should be doing anyway."[1] Let the dreams and ideas of others spark the flame in you. When they raise the bar, push it up a little higher through your own excellence.

Your passion, by the way, does not have to lie in the direct path of Christian ministry. God can use whatever you're zealous about. Maybe you love to strategize business plans, build circuit boards, or grow roses. Whatever it is, if you ask God, he'll show you how to use that love for him. I remember hearing about a man who sought out Rick Warren after reading *The Purpose Driven Life*. This man was a highly successful CEO of a globally known company, yet he was ready to give it all up to follow God. Rick showed him that God had a purpose for him right where he was, a ministry to accomplish within his company.

That's true for you, too. God wants to use you right where you are. You may or may not be working in your dream job. You may even feel discouraged about getting up and going to work every day. But imagine the story others could read through your life if you focused on being a light in their midst rather than a little black cloud. I'm not saying it's easy to know where God wants you. I am saying it's possible to find contentment and purpose where you are if you surrender every moment to God. When your heart is in his hands and your ears are open to his voice, then when he's ready to move you, you will know it.

If you haven't yet discovered the passion in your life, here are a few questions to ask yourself that might help you hear Jesus at the door:

- When you dream, where do your dreams generally drift?
- If money were not an obstacle and you could do anything for God, what would it would be?
- What is it that gets you off the couch?

The Passion Process

You might have to discover a few things about yourself to know what God wants you to share with others. For instance, once I'd discovered who God created me to be, I couldn't wait to help others make that same connection. Knowing that I get to do that almost every day helps me start each morning feeling that I'm doing something that matters for God, and I love every minute of it.

Stephanie has found it more of a process than an explosion. "I first have to discover who I am, what makes me tick, what I love, and who God has designed me to be before I can get a handle on my 'doing,'" she observed. "I don't think I'm completely there yet, but I do believe I'm finding contentment in the bigger piece of the puzzle of who I am."

In a letter I received from Jeff, he said, "For years I saw my job as just that . . . a job. Clock in at nine and leave at five. Day after day, it was the same old routine. After thirteen years of frustration, that routine ended the day I attended an Only You Can Be You conference that my church was hosting. I was challenged to give myself permission to embrace and express the talents and gifts God had given me. I learned I had to be a steward of what God had given me and that continuing to bury it was disobedient." Jeff opened himself to what God wanted him to do and has since discovered the rewards of being true to himself and to God's gifting and call. "I never thought a job could feel like play and be so rewarding," Jeff reports with enthusiasm about his new role. That's exactly how it feels when you're doing what God made you to do!

When we live in an attitude of surrender, God leads us gently and gradually. The living out of our passion may be at one level today, as it was for Kay Warren being a pastor's wife, and quite another a few years later, as when God stirred up a passion in her heart for the AIDS orphans.

You may have a dream that you don't think will ever come true. Let God surprise you. Expect him to, and he will.

One night a nondescript young man took the stage on a television show called *Britain's Got Talent.* It's a show much like *American Idol,* complete with Simon Cowell as a judge. Simon asked the young man who he was and what he wanted to do. "I sell mobile phones," he answered, "but I've always wanted to sing opera." Opera! The panel cringed, not sure what to expect, before Simon reluctantly invited him to go on. From the moment Paul Potts opened his mouth, the audience was on its feet. He sang with a clarity and exquisiteness comparable to that of the greatest opera legends. Because he dared to open himself up to what could be possible in his life, Paul Potts's dream has come true.

As we pursue the full potential God has placed within us, he reveals his plan for our lives. This is where we discover the unique individuals he made each of us to be. Only you can be you! Let God direct your dreams, and you will find your inner passion—or even your personal Paul Potts.

Whether your passion is something you're certain about and can't wait to get up and do every day or something you're slowly discovering one day at a time, the process is essentially the same. And each step takes you closer to living a life that counts.

Making It Count

Does God have a cause for you to conquer, or is there a need you are uniquely designed to meet? Believe it or not, God's answer is a resounding yes to at least one of those questions. If you seek him and listen for his voice, he will help you discover the answer. Let him stir your heart to action, and discover the challenge you were made to take on for him.

Whose needs are you best suited to meet? You may want to save the world, but that dream might be a little too big for one lifetime. Why not look at the needs God has met in your life and see if there isn't some way you can pass on that blessing to others. My guess is that he used other people in meeting your needs. Now you can be one of those need-meeters for someone else.

Can you see that this is just one more way in which God has made you for a unique purpose? Only you have experienced your life. Only you know the highs and lows, the successes and the lonely moments that have woven the distinctive tapestry of your life. While we are uniquely made, 1 Corinthians 10:13 tells us we are not uniquely tempted—that the nature of our experiences is universal. For that reason, your personal experience is bound to resonate with someone else and give hope to him or her in a difficult situation.

> He comforts us every time we have trouble,
> so when others have trouble, we can comfort
> them with the same comfort God gives us.
> 2 Corinthians 1:4 NCV

Today, reflect on the types of needs you can meet for others, and ask God to help you define your personal focus. Below are a few types of needs you might consider.

1. Educational needs, best met by those who enjoy training, teaching, and developing others.
2. Emotional needs, best met by those who enjoy counseling.

3. Relational needs, best met by those who discover their passion in helping people connect.

4. Material needs, best met by those who simply want to help someone in need.

5. Spiritual needs, best met by those who long to help others discover a personal relationship with Christ.

6. Vocational needs, best met by those with the expertise to train or coach others to reach professional goals.

As you reflect, ask yourself what needs you most love to meet, why you love to meet them, and what life lessons you could pass on to someone else. You'll discover many possibilities! The key question to ask is, where can my life make the biggest impact for God? The added bonus is that when you are operating out of your God-given passions, you won't feel like you're working at all.

Let's offer this prayer together.

Father, I long to know what you made me to do. There are so many possibilities! Help me to know through your divine reassurance that the direction I am headed in is the right one and that whether or not I am currently in a position that is geared toward fulfilling your design, you will use it as another building block in my life—taking me to that place you've already picked out for me. As I review this material and seek to understand what needs you want me to meet, help me to be open to your surprises and to let your Spirit guide me in the way that I should go. In Jesus' name, amen.

When we meet again tomorrow, we'll look at how your life experiences work together with your abilities, your spiritual gifts, your passion, and your design to make you uniquely you. Believe it or not, even your pain has a purpose.

Day 12

ROLLER COASTER

Using Your Ups and Downs

Character cannot be developed in ease and quiet. Only through experience of trial and suffering can the soul be strengthened, ambition inspired, and success achieved.
—Helen Keller

We know that in all things God works for the good of those who love him, who have been called according to his purpose.
Romans 8:28

The purpose of life, after all, is to live it, to taste experience to the utmost, to reach out eagerly and without fear for newer and richer experiences.
—Eleanor Roosevelt

HAVE YOU EVER FELT that your life is like an elevator ride in a twenty-story building? One day you're at the top and the next you've hit bottom. Every life has its ups and downs. Just when you think you've reached the top, you find yourself going down. But when you know God, you can also know that there is purpose in every start and stop, every floor, every person who joins you.

Years ago Janet answered God's call to "feed my sheep" when she began a mentoring ministry for the women at her church. She could not have known at that time how God planned to prepare her to identify with the needs of these women. Since her call, Janet has survived a formidable battle with breast cancer. With the joy born of obedience, she speaks about her experience, offering hope and help to women in similar circumstances. She also has experienced the pain of separation from a daughter who wandered from the faith in which she'd been raised. Drawing on memories of her own youth and on her experience that enables her to relate to thousands of other praying parents, Janet has written a book, *Praying for Your Prodigal Daughter*. Further, she and her husband regularly open their home to people seeking support and hope regarding their prodigal children.

Our lives don't have to be filled with drama or pain for God to use our experiences. We simply must yield our lives—whatever our circumstances and experiences—to his purposes. Someone, somewhere, needs the help only you can give—the message only you can bring.

Going Up?

When you think back on all the moments of your life, which do you consider the high points? These are clues to which kinds of pursuits will deliver the greatest satisfaction, helping you to fully become the person God made you to be.

This analysis should be not so much about how others perceive what you've done but how you see it. Those achievements that have brought you true joy are almost always those in which God also delights. Does that surprise you? Allow yourself to take pleasure in what God loves about you!

Why not make a map of your life, listing those high points? Think about them in light of your personal achievements, your educational victories, your relational wins, your spiritual triumphs, and your vocational accomplishments. Make a list in the space provided, and see if you can single out a few highlights in your life. This exercise will help you see those times when God has lifted you to what felt like the mountaintop. Remember what you saw and felt and heard while you were there, and zero in on what gave you the highest high. Ask God to help you understand how you can use these moments to build something unique and lasting in your life that will also serve the needs of others.

High Points in My Life

My wife, Stacey, inspires me. While my childhood resembled *The Addams Family,* hers was more of a continuous loop of *7th Heaven* episodes. But rather than become a bored or a desperate housewife, she has taken those positive memories and put them to use on behalf of our kids. I am grateful for this amazing woman who daily teaches me how to love others and listen for God's voice. My relationship with Stacey is, without a doubt, one of the high points of my life.

Being able to use your achievements and experiences for God is not subject to any age limit. As a senior citizen, Gene got fired up about helping others reach new heights with God in their lives. One morning he said to his brother-in-law, "I wish there were a way to help senior citizens pass on their knowledge to their children and grandchildren, whether or not they lived nearby." Gene shared his idea with his pastor and subsequently developed a ministry teaching seniors how to have a positive influence on the younger people in their lives. "It has reignited the seniors in this church and is having a life-changing effect on hundreds of grandchildren," said one man who has witnessed this move of the Spirit firsthand.

Going Down

Perhaps you've heard it said that for every high there must be a low. Our elevator lives bear this out—some more than others.

Horatio Spafford was a prominent Chicago attorney. A Christian, he had gained a reputation as a supporter of evangelist D. L. Moody. Then Spafford's four-year-old son contracted scarlet fever and died. A year later, the Great Chicago Fire of 1871 wiped out his substantial real-estate holdings.

In 1873, Spafford planned to take his wife and daughter on a holiday in England. Just before their steamship was to depart, a last-minute business deal delayed Spafford. He sent his wife and daughters on ahead, with plans to meet them later. A short time later, Spafford received a telegram from his wife. The French steamer on which they'd sailed had collided with an English vessel, sinking the French ship in a matter of minutes. Mrs. Spafford had been spared when a plank from the ship floated under her and supported her unconscious body, but not so their four daughters. Her heartbreaking telegram to her husband read: "Saved alone."

Horatio Spafford had known life's highs, and now he was suffering the lowest of its lows. En route to join his grieving wife, passing by the very spot where his daughters had died in the chilly waters of the Atlantic, Spafford wrote a hymn that showed his abiding faith in God, which had carried him through his ordeals. He recognized that God's eternal goodness was not based on temporary circumstances, and so he wrote, "Whatever my lot, Thou hast taught me to say, 'It is well, it is well with my soul.'"

Today we don't remember the cases Spafford tried or how many properties he owned, but our Christian heritage is richer for this beautiful hymn—"It Is Well with My Soul"—written in the depths of his personal despair. If we want our lives to count, we must be willing to recognize that hard times are part of God's design for us. Whether you've suffered loss, as Horatio Spafford did; or illness, like Janet; or abuse, depression, bankruptcy, abortion, or any other of life's excruciating sorrows; God wants to use it as part of his plan to mold you into the image of his Son. Life's crises can become God's channels if we'll simply choose to tune in to him whenever our cries of pain threaten to drown him out.

Sandra made that choice. Following is her story.

It was too early in the morning for visitors. *Who could be at the door?* she wondered. "Are you Sandra?" the police officers asked. "We're sorry to have to tell you that your daughter Tiffany was killed last night in an automobile crash."

No! How could this happen? Why would God take my baby?

In an instant, Sandra's well-ordered life was turned completely upside down and inside out. Just days earlier, Sandra and her husband had sent Tiffany off to school in Kentucky, full of plans to pursue her dream of a writing career. Surely this couldn't be part of God's plan for her life. But Sandra's small Bible-study group had just finished a forty-day study of God's purposes. As a believer and a Bible teacher, she felt certain that God didn't let accidents happen. She determined to "get in God's face and stay there" until he revealed to her what he possibly could have in mind by allowing this tragedy.

Days crawled into months as Sandra attempted in vain to pull herself out of her deep grief. In time God would comfort her with visions of Tiffany dancing before his throne and ideas for how Sandra could continue her daughter's legacy. Today Sandra leads a ministry dedicated to young mothers Tiffany's age, and she has plans to publish a children's book series written in her daughter's memory.

God can use even our deepest pain if we surrender it into his hands.

Gary learned this lesson too. After years of trying and failing and trying again to make their marriage work, his wife had had enough. When she left, Gary was devastated. A friend invited him to a men's retreat, and having nothing better to do that weekend, he went. How could he have known what God had in mind? At that event Gary turned his life over to the Lord. Within months he'd begun an outreach to other men in marital crisis. Although Gary was not able to restore his marriage, God did bring him a new love. Happily remarried, Gary continues to use the lessons of his first marriage to teach and encourage others in their relationship struggles.

Your Story

A friend once asked me, referring to the pain of my childhood, "Don't you ever wish you'd never experienced that pain?" Of course I would love to have had a happy childhood, but I recognize that without my life being exactly as it was, I'd be far less equipped to help others find God's unique plan for their lives. Pain is part of the story of our lives.

Think of the day Jesus appointed Peter to care for his flock. He hinted at the difficulties that lay ahead for Peter: " 'I tell you the truth, when you were younger you dressed yourself and went where you wanted; but when you are old you will stretch out your hands, and someone else will dress you and lead you where you do not want to go.' Jesus said this to indicate the kind of death by which Peter would glorify God. Then he said to him, 'Follow me!'" (John 21:18–19).

Like a jealous brother, Peter pointed to John and said, " 'Lord, what about him?' Jesus answered, 'If I want him to remain alive until I return, what is that to you? You must follow me'" (John 21:21–22).

God has a unique story for *your* life. It's not the same as my story, or Gary's, or Sandra's, or Janet's, or Horatio Spafford's. It's not the same as Peter's story, either. Your story is unique to you—both the high points and the lows—and God wants to use it all. He won't do it, however, without your permission. That leaves the choice up to you: will you let your life display his glory?

As you did with the high points, take some time right now to identify some of the lowest moments in your life. Then release them to God and ask him to make something beautiful from them.

Low Points in My Life

Making It Count

At age seventeen, Karen found herself pregnant and getting married to her child's father, a man five years older than she. For Karen and John, a situation that would have ranked as a lifetime low for many young couples turned out to have a happy ending. "By the grace of God and with a lot of work and love, we have been married for thirteen years now," Karen said, "and we have three beautiful girls." As for using her experiences, Karen reported: "I have realized my passion for teens, specifically girls facing the same situation I was in all those years ago.

I long to either help them when they have become pregnant or help them learn how to avoid finding themselves in that situation." Karen is pursuing a counseling degree and is researching ways to put the wisdom she has gained through her painful experiences to work on behalf of young women. When she thinks about where God wants to use her, Karen says she becomes energized, and she has even teamed up with a close friend who shares her passion to help these teens. Their dreams are still in the beginning stages, but together they plan to bring hope into the lives of young girls in their community.

"Our hearts burn bright to bring these girls hope, wisdom, and direction. They need to know that this isn't the end of their dreams, it's just a step in the process. I want my legacy to be changing and empowering the legacy of others."

As eager as Karen is to get started on this adventure, she recognizes that God can use her right where she is, right now.

"I know that my job is a part of my purpose right now. I'm there to shine God's light, even if it doesn't seem to have as profound an impact as counseling troubled teens would. I'm biding my time until God chooses to change my arena of ministry."

Karen recognizes that in all things, God works for the good of those who love him—even in our troubles or in times of waiting and preparation. Karen believes that all these things are working out God's purposes in her life.

At the beginning of this chapter, we looked at Romans 8:28. Let's review it one more time in light of all the ups and downs we've been discussing. Here's how the Message puts it: "The moment we get tired in the waiting, God's Spirit is right alongside helping us along. If we don't know how or what to pray, it doesn't matter. He does our praying in and for us, making prayer out of our wordless sighs, our aching groans. He knows us far better than we know ourselves, knows our pregnant condition, and keeps us present before God. That's why we can be so sure that every detail in our lives of love for God is worked into something good" (Romans 8:28).

Are you willing to give God every aspect of your life and let him turn it into something good? Maybe you thought you'd put away those hurts for good, and now you're feeling a little resentful at having to live with them again. Let me assure you that if you trust in God and let him have both your ups and your downs, you'll discover a rich life you never could have planned for yourself—and it will be a life that counts.

If this sounds like we're talking about surrender all over again, it's because, in a sense, we are. Surrender is not a onetime thing. It's a daily process. In her book *Dangerous Surrender,* Kay Warren writes about the Kingdom of Me—a place we all know well. We all live there. But in order to let God rule over our lives, we must yield our right to the throne and let him establish his kingdom in our hearts. No one said it would be easy.

Today, take those lists you made of the highs and lows in your life and ask God to use them. Then, expect him to do it. Let him operate the elevator of life, and you can rest assured that the ride will always end well—well with your soul.

Let's pray together.

Father, help us to see that you long to use every moment of our lives, the good along with the bad, to build your kingdom for all eternity. Give us the courage to face what has gone wrong in our lives, and help us to see that you are still good. You are the author of our lives, and your plan is for the story to end well. It's why you sent Jesus, in whose name we pray. Amen.

When we meet back here tomorrow, we'll look at the special personality God has programmed inside you. Did you know that he even has a special plan for your kookiness? It's all part of the you that only you can be.

Day 13

SEASONINGS

Flavoring Life with Your Personal Style

What comes into our minds when we think about God
is the most important thing about us.
—A. W. Tozer

The human body has many parts, but the many parts make up
one whole body. So it is with the body of Christ. . . . We have all
been baptized into one body by one Spirit, and we all share the
same Spirit. . . . Our bodies have many parts, and God
has put each part just where he wants it.
1 Corinthians 12:12, 13, 18 NLT

D o you like to cook? Even if you don't, I'll bet you enjoy food,
so you'll relate to my friend Shaun's lesson. He and his wife have a
great agreement. He loves to cook and she loves to clean, so they each do
what they like best, and it keeps their home perfectly seasoned with peace
and harmony. Not long ago Shaun made a YouTube video in which he
describes the experience of cooking fried rice for his family. He didn't do
this for the Food Channel but to offer a unique perspective on how God
made us. The key to successful rice, he explains, is in the ingredients. As
you add your favorite seasonings, you bring out a special flavor that sets
your friend rice apart.

God used special seasonings in making you, and it's those ingredients that bring out the flavor of Christ. He also has seasoned you with a one-of-a-kind flavor—what we call your personality. It's what makes you you, and God wants to use it to draw others into his presence through you. The good news is, you don't have to be a five-star-restaurant entrée to be used by God in this way. You just have to be who God made you to be.

Spicy, Salty, Sweet: Personality Types That Flavor Our Lives

Are you hot and spicy, cool as a cucumber, bold as brass, or timid? God has a purpose in every personality trait, and it all adds up to make you the distinct person you are. Your personality is knitted together from your mental, spiritual, and moral qualities, all of which combine to form your character.

Psychologists and behavior specialists love to categorize people by personality types. You may have heard of these well-known temperament types: melancholy (creative, moody), sanguine (fun-loving, often wild), phlegmatic (calm, even disposition), and choleric (strong-willed). Christian counselor and family relationship expert John Trent compares us to animals, using the beaver, otter, golden retriever, and lion to describe different personality types.[1]

Perhaps you've heard of or taken one of the personality-assessment profiles popular in today's workplace settings, like the Myers-Briggs Type Indicator or the True Colors Test. Each of these seeks to help us understand one another and ourselves in order to help us relate better on the job or in the home.

The point is, God has wired each of us in a slightly different way to make sure his message connects with as many people as possible. One of my favorite tools for understanding how this works is the "thinking wavelength," developed by my friend Tom Paterson, the author.[2] Tom examines five predominant thinking patterns. Essentially, there are efficiency experts, the people who get the work done; concrete thinkers, those who can manage teams of people; proprietors, who could run the whole store single-handedly; scouts, capable of visionary thinking and gifted at discovering new talent; and scientists, best suited for teaching at universities or working in laboratories. No particular way of thinking is better or worse than another. We're simply made differently and on purpose.

Making assessments of personality types can be a lot of fun. They can also be a convenient way to better understand our natural tendencies and those of others. But they should never be an excuse for our failures and immoderations. Have you ever heard, or even said yourself, "I can't help it! It's just the way I am!" Or, "I'm hot-tempered like my Irish grandmother" or, "I'm a sanguine—you can't expect me to follow through on my commitments." What excuses we come up with to justify our bad behavior. We live in a society that has become more about our rights than about our responsibilities. While it all sounds good, what do you suppose God thinks about this?

God longs to use us just as he made us, but that doesn't give us carte blanche to exhibit poor behavior. The goal is to bring our personality types under God's direction. When we submit ourselves to the orchestration of the Holy Spirit, it's amazing how God can channel, refine, redirect, and polish our natural tendencies to be better and more effective. Like an orchestra tuning up, what may sound like a caterwaul when we play our own tune in our own time can, with God's help and discipline, become a symphony for God when we follow the lead of the Master Conductor.

Saul was a type-A personality—a lion; a choleric; a bold, spicy flavor—who persecuted Christians with unmatched zeal. God changed Saul's heart, not his personality. And Paul (God changed his name, too) became a type-A lion, choleric, bold-spicy zealot for God. He became, arguably, the most effective tool for God's kingdom in the history of the church. God used Paul's personality and natural gifts for good, setting them free to flourish.

Much can be done for the kingdom of heaven, and God wants to use all of us to accomplish his mission. Don't get me wrong: he doesn't *need* us to reach his goals. Using us is a privilege he extends to us because he loves us. The point is that he desires to partner with us. Every time I think of it—the king of heaven has chosen me!—the very idea drives me to my knees in gratitude.

God has given us spiritual gifts, abilities, passionate interests, experiences, and even the peculiarities of our personalities to steward for him on this earth. They are not "rights" but an awesome responsibility.

Blending Personal Flavors for Maximum Impact

When we look at Jesus' disciples, we find an amazing mix of personalities. There was bold and brash Peter, sometimes speaking before thinking, ready to cut off the ear of one who tried to arrest his Master. And there was quiet, faithful John. Matthew had served as a tax collector, so we can imagine he might have been a little hard-nosed. Or maybe he was a quiet, precise accountant type. Thomas, the doubter, seems like a loyal pessimist. (In John 11:16, when Jesus proposed going to Judea even though the religious leaders there were trying to kill him, Thomas said, "Let us also go, that we may die with him.") Nathanael was a skeptic. Simon was a Zealot, a member of a radical, sometimes violent, political party. Yet Jesus loved them all. He called them and appointed them to carry out his Great Commission because he knew they were just the right people for the job. He could count on them. Can he count on you?

What's your personal flavor?

- Are you the life of the party or are you quiet?
- Do you express your thoughts easily or keep them to yourself?
- Do you go along with the crowd or compete to be the best?
- When it comes to opportunities, are you drawn to those whom others find impossible to love, or are you hard to budge from your comfortable rut?

- Do you love projects that involve lots of people contact, or do you prefer to work alone?
- Are you people-oriented or task-oriented?
- Am I likely to find you out front, leading the group, or somewhere in the pack, hoping you can do what is asked of you?
- Do you enjoy being a team member or do you work best as an individual contributor?
- Are you happy with the same old thing, day in and day out, with as little change as possible, or do you like to mix it up a little?

All these answers reveal your unique personality blend. The more you understand about that, the better you'll be able to steward your personality traits for God and work with him in creating the most delicious you possible.

One day Michelle dropped into my office for advice. "I don't have an 'out-front' personality," she said. "Does that make me less important?" I explained to her that God doesn't measure us in terms of aggressive or passive personality traits, or by position or possessions. God is more interested in those less-apparent aspects of our lives. Are we trustworthy, loyal, dependable, kind? Do we seek to serve others before we serve ourselves? Those are the characteristics God values.

Today Michelle is happy serving behind the scenes, using the gifts and personality God entrusted to her. She is stewarding her unique personality in God-pleasing ways, and she's discovering that God loves behind-the-scenes personalities just as much as he loves extroverts. Where would we be without the behind-the-scenes people? Those jobs need to get done, or nothing gets done. Besides, there is no "behind the scenes" with God. He sees it all. He knows what we do for him in the dark, small, unseen places. And he cares.

It has been said that character is what we are when we think no one is watching. Your character determines how you relate to others and how you respond to the opportunities that come your way in life. Are you honest and aboveboard in your dealings at all times? If not, why not? Would others call you reliable? Dependable? Someone they can count on in a pinch? When a door opens for you, do you go through it without a second thought, or do you consider first what might be on the other side? Do you weigh your options, or do you charge full steam ahead?

No matter what your strengths or tendencies are, God has designed you in that way in order to reach certain people for Christ. Part of accepting this aspect of your personality is to thank him for everyone he brings across your path. It's not your job to figure out for whom or how he will use you but simply to be you and to be available for him to use when and in the way he sees fit.

Not Bland in God's Book

Still don't particularly like the way God made you? Do you wish your "flavor" were a little spicier, a little more noticeable, a little more outstanding? Disappointed with the realization that you're really quite ordinary? Don't be. In God's book, "ordinary" can be extraordinary. Everyone is someone special to God. All of us are capable of great things when we do the things to which God has called us.

Kay Warren recalls how, as a little girl, she wanted to be Cinderella—a real princess. Many little girls share that dream. Then, as the young wife of an energetic pastor, she wanted to be dynamic—a star in her own right. What she finally realized is that she is, in fact, just average. A lot of us see ourselves that way, as just ordinary or average—not voted team captain, homecoming king or queen, or most likely to succeed. Secretly we might wish we could be celebrities or really special people on the world stage. But the fact is, few of us are superstars.

Such a revelation could drive us to despair, or we can choose to see ourselves through God's eyes. Consider what God did through "ordinary" men like Jesus' disciples. After Jesus had ascended to heaven and the church was officially born, Peter and John witnessed to large audiences of people, explaining to them about Jesus' ministry, death, and resurrection and healing people in Jesus' name. When Peter and John healed a crippled beggar at the temple gate, the astonished crowd came running to see what had happened and to listen to Peter and John speak about Jesus. Not surprisingly, the local Jewish leaders—who had thought they had gotten rid of Jesus once and for all—were not happy about this. They had Peter and John thrown in jail overnight. The next day, before the Sanhedrin (the Jewish high court), Peter and John were asked, "By what power or what name did you do this?" (Acts 4:7). The story goes on:

> Then Peter, filled with the Holy Spirit, said to them: "Rulers and elders of the people! If we are being called to account today for an act of kindness shown to a cripple and are asked how he was healed, then know this, you and all the people of Israel: It is by the name of Jesus Christ of Nazareth, whom you crucified but whom God raised from the dead, that this man stands before you healed. He is 'the stone you builders rejected, which has become the capstone.' Salvation is found in no one else, for there is no other name under heaven given to men by which we must be saved."
>
> When they saw the courage of Peter and John and realized that they were unschooled, *ordinary* men, they were astonished and they took note that these men had been with Jesus. But since they could see the man who had been healed standing there with them, there was nothing they could say" (Acts 4:8–14, emphasis added).

Just as he did with Peter and John and with Paul, James, Matthew, Mark, Luke, and so many others down through history—as he is doing with Kay Warren today—so God wants to do extraordinary works through your life. Remember, he used wonderful, heavenly ingredients when he created you. Give him permission to serve them up in ways that multiply his kingdom.

Making It Count

Can you smell what's cooking? God is the master chef of your life, and he wants you, his creation du jour, to make the most of the ingredients he's poured into you in ways that maximize the flavor and appeal.

It's critical to understand your personality if you're going to pursue a life that aligns with the way God made you. Don't try to be someone you're not or force yourself into a mold that just doesn't fit you. It's okay to be you!

To help you separate the salt from the pepper, take some time today to rate yourself in a few of the categories we've discussed. You may find that you are completely one way or another or that you fall somewhere in between. What matters is that you accept the person God made you to be—whoever that may be. I've seen people try to be stars when God made them to be stagehands. If you've ever watched the credits go by on the movie screen, you know it takes all those people to get the show on the road. So don't worry if God didn't call you to be a missionary or the leader of a great crusade. He called you to do something that no one else can do nearly as well as you can: be you.

Are you . . .

1. An efficiency expert, known for getting the job done?
2. A concrete thinker who efficiently manages teams?
3. A proprietor, able to run the whole store single-handedly?
4. A scout, always full of new ideas and looking for the right people to make your dreams come true?
5. A scientist, born for professorship or laboratory experimentation?

Pray about what the answers mean for you and about you, and thank God for making you according to his special recipe. Write your thoughts in the space provided.

Let's tell God we're ready to get cooking.

Lord, thank you for making me as you have, quirky ingredients and all. I confess that in the past, I've complained about that combination. It seems to be human nature to be dissatisfied with the way we are. But I now realize that you are my maker, and you made me this way because it pleased you to do so. Help me to put those crazy components to work in this world for you—no excuses, just full-bodied flavor for Jesus. It's in his name I pray. . . . Amen.

All this week we've been looking at all the wonderful gifts God has given you to steward for him. Tomorrow we'll find out what happens when we determine to make good use of all those gifts by taking hold of our life purpose.

INSIDE THE BOX

Discovering the True You

Take delight in the LORD,
and he will give you your heart's desires.
Psalm 37:4 NLT

It is the first of all problems for a man to find out
what kind of work he is to do in this universe.
—Thomas Carlyle

H AVE YOU EVER PUT together a jigsaw puzzle? You take the box, dump the pieces out on the floor or a table, and then try to figure out how to put them together. This past week we've been looking at the various elements God has placed inside us like puzzle pieces in a box. Now it's time to look at them all together so that next week we can discover how God wants to use the completed puzzles that we are to bless others.

It's one thing to know that we have been given abilities, spiritual gifts, a lifetime of experiences, an original personality, and a passion for solving a particular problem or serving a special group. But none of these, on its own, answers that big question we started with: Who am I?

It's a question that has haunted mankind throughout the ages. We despair over it, we go on quests to find the answer, we stuff ourselves full of substitutes for finding the real us, or, worse, we completely ignore the question.

In his book *Living a Life on Loan,* Rick Rusaw recalls how, as children, he and his sister used their mother's jigsaw puzzles for purposes other than the manufacturer's intention. They would put pieces from several boxes on the floor and use them for sliding across the floor. It was all great fun until it came time to put the pieces back in their proper boxes. That's when they discovered that, to their dismay, there was no telling where those little pieces actually belonged.

"Sometimes your life may look like an insignificant cardboard piece," Rusaw writes, "not even a border piece or one with an obvious place to fit into. You might even think some of the puzzle pieces in your box belong in other boxes! You wonder what good this life is—not much value, not much significance, nearly useless. But this is God's picture, his puzzle. He knows what he's doing. If the Bible is right, then God indicates that your part of the puzzle is needed, valued, and planned for."[1]

All of us wonder from time to time why we're here and where we could possibly fit in the big picture. But God wants us to know that our part of the puzzle is definitely important. In one-on-one coaching sessions and in seminars the world over, I've been privileged to witness the wonder of people discovering this truth. The key, they discover, is to "stay within the box." That sounds like bad advice, considering all the talk we hear these days about thinking "outside the box." But the only way to know what God has planned for us is to look inside the boxes that we are and discover all that God has packed in there to use for serving others.

Imagine that you've just received a package from God. If you pull up the flaps, take out all the Styrofoam peanuts, and look inside, what will you see in terms of gifts, talents, passion, experiences, and personality that God might have handpicked to complete the puzzle of you? I hope this week has helped you discover what's in your box so that you can begin to clarify who you are and develop confidence in what God has in store for you.

Unpacking Your Box

What has God been showing you about your design? Are you starting to see the picture on the front of the puzzle box of what you may someday be? As you look back on our discussions of this past week, are you able to see more clearly how God might want to use the talents he gave you? Can you identify at least one spiritual gift you feel God has given you? How about those moments when you know Jesus is knocking at the door of your heart? And how might he use those experiences that have marked the road map of your life so far? Whom can he touch through your Master-designed personality?

As you consider these questions, it's time to roll up your sleeves and get to work assembling the puzzle of the real you. Following are some practical steps you can take today to see those pieces start falling into place.

Sort the Pieces

Anyone with puzzle experience knows that one of the first steps in putting one together is to sort the pieces: edge pieces here, reds in this pile, sky pieces over there, building pieces in another place, and people or animals somewhere else. Organizing the pieces makes it a whole lot easier to make sense of the hundreds of tiny, similar shapes. As we've shared coffee over the past few days, you've made lists of some of those pieces. Now I want you to flip back through the pages and use those lists to make a new one here. If you can see those pieces all together, like puzzle pieces on the floor, you might begin to see how they could fit together to make something for God—something only you can make.

My strongest talents are_____.

My spiritual gift(s) are_____.

I am passionate about_____.

I can relate to someone else because I've been through_____

_____.

I best relate to others as a(n) [efficiency expert, concrete thinker, proprietor, scout, scientist]_____.

Find the Outside Edges

Finding—and piecing together—the outside edges is perhaps the best and easiest way to launch your successful puzzle-making endeavor. Not only are the straight-edged pieces easiest to find, they give your entire project definition. They limit the scope of the puzzle and let you know approximately where the inside sections belong—sky up near the top, grass below, trees pointing up, this mountain over here. Establishing the limits—the outer edges—guides and gives form to our efforts, whether we're putting together a puzzle or piecing together our God-given purpose.

How do you find the edges of your purpose? Determine what needs God is asking you to meet. Survey once more those pieces in your box. Are there specific needs you can meet through your talents, your gifts, your passion, your experiences, or your personality? How can you use all he gave you to meet the needs of others?

Put People First

Puzzle makers know: skies are vast and difficult. They sometimes look like water. It's much easier to piece together people. People are distinct. The figures are unique. They have faces that speak to us and help us distinguish one from another. The easiest, most fulfilling part of any puzzle is putting together the figures of people. That's perhaps the easiest, most fulfilling part of discovering the ministry for which God has gifted and prepared us, too. Which people is God enabling you to reach for him? Whose lives are you equipped to help piece back together with God's help?

John was a recovering alcoholic who saw that the pieces in his box could impact other alcoholics for Christ. That isn't something God has equipped or prepared me to do, but John is perfect for it. God took

John's vision and multiplied it. His Celebrate Recovery program began at Saddleback Church and now serves churches around the globe, transforming alcoholics, drug addicts, people with codependency issues, and all manner of addictions. John responded in gratitude to what God had done for him by reaching out to help others who were in the same kind of trouble. He used the gifts God gave him to develop and grow a life-changing ministry that is now benefiting thousands of people and their families. God is accomplishing his purposes through John.

God is in the people business, so your purpose is likely to be serving a specific target audience for him, as John is doing. So whom is God calling you to help? Is it the elderly or the very young? Executives or co-workers? Believers or those who need to hear the gospel's message of hope? Men? Women? Find the target group of people—the audience—that God made you to serve in ways only you can. Why not take a step of faith right now and write down a few possibilities in the space below. Think back to our conversation on Day 11—where do you hear Jesus knocking on your heart? It's likely that your intended audience is somewhere in that place.

People I Will Serve for God

-
-
-

Set a Strategy for Finishing

Once you've begun putting all those pieces in your box together and have gotten them working for God, probably the hardest thing you'll have to do is harness the excitement you'll have for meeting so many needs. It's easy to get burned out in ministry, but that's all the more reason to find your personal focus. What specific needs does God want you to meet, and which can be better met by others? To help you find that focus, try volunteering on ministry teams whenever you can. Great teams pull together so that no one person is doing all the work. And every puzzle worker knows it's far easier to finish a puzzle when you work on it with a team. What is too overwhelming for one person can be more easily handled and brought to completion by several people working together.

Is the picture of God's plan for you beginning to take shape? Take time right now to hold those pieces up to God, as you did symbolically with your life at the end of last week. Surrender them to him, and as you do, ask him for just enough light to see your next steps. God rarely shows us the whole picture of our lives, but when we understand that he longs to use us just the way he made us, we can begin to trust him to complete the picture in his own time and way. Our job is to continually offer him all the pieces in our boxes.

Celebrating the Completed Puzzle

The Bible tells us we can place our confidence in God because he is the one working through us: "We can say this, because through Christ we feel certain before God. We are not saying that we can do this work ourselves. It is God who makes us able to do all that we do" (2 Corinthians 3:4–5 NCV). It tells us that if we trust in God with all our hearts rather than depend on our own understanding, and if we truly seek to please him and do his will, he will show us which path we should take (Proverbs 3:5–6 NLT).

Are you ready to activate God's plan for your life? One great way to begin is by celebrating his presence in your life. The apostle Paul encouraged believers to "celebrate God all day, every day. I mean, revel in him! Make it as clear as you can to all you meet that you're on their side, working with them and not against them. Help them see that the Master is about to arrive. He could show up any minute!" (Philippians 4:4 MSG).

God's dream for you is better than anything you could imagine on your own. He challenges you to dream big and then expect him to do even more than you imagined. Paul declared: "All glory to God, who is able, through his mighty power at work within us, to accomplish infinitely more than we might ask or think" (Ephesians 3:20 NLT).

In his book *Experiencing God,* Henry Blackaby gives us this reassurance: "Whenever God gives you a directive, it is always right. God's will is always best. You never have to question whether His will is best or right. It is always best and right. This is true because He loves you and knows all. Because He loves you perfectly, you can trust Him and obey Him completely. Not only is God loving and all-knowing, but He also is all-powerful. No matter how big the assignment He gives you, He is able to accomplish His purposes through you."[2] No matter how big! Does that thought excite you about using what's in your box? God will accomplish his purposes through you!

Inside Edition: One Woman's Puzzle

Remember Debbie from Day 9, who became a high achiever to prove wrong the school counselor who wrote off her chances of success in college and in life? Debbie worked hard at a clothing store in the mall, and her life took off from there. A deeper look into her story helps us to see just how God puts all the pieces together for his glory.

When Debbie tells her story, she always begins with that starting point in her childhood—when the teachers and counselors told her she was slow or that she had learning difficulties and to forget about college. Painful memories like these could have crippled her and kept her from becoming the person God created her to be.

But because she invited God into her life, she can now look back and see his handiwork in the tapestry, patiently stitching away even before she knew him. Today, she is well on her way to making the most of the life God gave her. With God's help, Debbie has figured out how to put all the pieces together.

In the middle of her climb up the corporate ladder, Debbie and her husband decided it was time to start a family. But, try as they might, that dream was denied again and again. Then, during a job transition, she finally became pregnant!

But Debbie lost the baby.

"At that point," Debbie recalls, "my husband and I were not walking with the Lord. I woke up out of a dead sleep one Sunday morning, turned to my husband, and said, 'I need to go to church.' He said, 'Where are we going?' I didn't know. An hour later, a friend from work called and said, 'Debbie, you've got to go to my church today. The sermon is perfect for what you just went through.'" The message was "When God Says Yes, No, or Maybe" and featured testimonies from three infertile couples. "We recommitted our lives to God that day," Debbie said.

Still, several more years passed before God would answer the prayers of Debbie and her husband. Finally they reached a crossroads with Debbie's career. Her job was moving: should she transfer to a new location or leave her position? Debbie laid down her job—and discovered that she was pregnant again. Three weeks after her role as a professional ended, she took up the mantle of Mom.

"It rocked my world. I mean, I was a corporate woman—you work hard to achieve that! Looking back, I realize that my identity was in my job. Now everything had been stripped away. It was just me and my baby and my husband, living in a world I knew nothing about." She missed the corporate woman she no longer was. But, in a spirit of obedience to what she felt God was asking of her at that particular time, she stayed home with her young son and began volunteering at her church.

"I now realize God was doing an enormous amount of work in me and my character in those five years that I stayed home with my little boy," Debbie explained. "He had to take me through some character transformation before he would allow me to move into a role that would use the talents and skills and gifts he had given me to do his work. I was confident that my identity was in Christ and he would equip me. Now I can see how he prepared me to lead women at my church, because in the business world I'd learned about conflict resolution, negotiation, flexibility, resourcefulness, people skills, and leading people. He just had to take me out of being in the center, to being a mom, where you give up the focus on yourself. He used all those skills from the workplace to bring me to the workplace I'm in now."

Debbie now sees how all the puzzle pieces of her life fit together, and she celebrates every day by using those pieces to serve God by serving others. You can see all the scattered, disparate pieces of the puzzle of your life come together like that, too. And when you get there, you'll want to celebrate.

Making It Count

We serve a God of supernatural power, but being a Christian isn't about being weird or living a sheltered life away from others or having a phony mystical aura operating in our lives. God does most of his supernatural work in us using completely natural means. That makes discovering our purpose easier than we might think. In fact, when we understand how it works and see it in action a time or two, we'll wonder why it took this long to figure it out.

God has put inside you a love for doing certain things that will meet the needs of specific people. The only part you really have to work to figure out is how you're going to do it. How will you serve God, and where? To find the answers, pick up those pieces that reveal your abilities, your experiences, and your personality. What do you most enjoy doing? Where have you had your most fulfilling times? With whom did you work best? What kinds of opportunities appeal to you most?

Spend time today reflecting on those questions. Journal your answers to help you see the picture more clearly.

Finally, figure out what services you can best provide and where. Are you a teacher, a counselor, an expert authority; or are you a doer—someone who serves physical needs, like a doctor or a physical therapist? Will you likely be most effective one-on-one or addressing a large group from a stage?

When you look at all the pieces in your box, what is the puzzle shaping up to look like?

If you need more help seeing the big picture, email me so I can help you put the final pieces together. I would also encourage you again to test-drive a few possibilities. Experiment with various opportunities to serve at your church or in your community. One of the best things about volunteering is that it's not like a job. When we pursue career opportunities, we're often at the mercy of employers who either set us up to succeed or pigeonhole us. As a volunteer you're free to try just about anything and find the best fit for you.

Where can you begin serving this week? Jot down a few possibilities as they occur to you, and pray about how you will put your puzzle pieces together for God. If you're already serving, take inventory with God to find out if this is the best fit for you. Is there a door opening somewhere that you should consider going through?

Only you can be you, and only you can serve God in exactly the way he has in mind. You were made to make a difference with your life. What difference are the contents of your box likely to make? For the best results, follow the Manufacturer's guidelines.

Let's pray together.

Lord, thank you for all the wonderful ways in which you have made us. Give us eyes to see how we are to put this amazing puzzle together so that when we are done, we will look like the people you made each of us to be instead of someone else. Help us to see and to seize our purpose today, as Jesus did when he came to earth. It's in his name we pray. Amen.

Tomorrow we'll begin a week of looking at the ultimate purpose for your life—to serve others through the uniqueness that is you. Let's meet back here tomorrow for a singularly great cup of coffee and a deeper insight into what God was thinking when he made you.

LIFE CHOICE 3

*Serve Others
Passionately*

Day 15

APRON

Loving through Serving

I am among you as one who serves.
Luke 22:27

If you wish to be a leader you will be frustrated,
for very few people wish to be led. If you aim to be a servant,
you will never be frustrated.
—Frank F. Warren

THEY'D EXPECTED A KING, dressed in rich robes and living in a splendid castle. He would come, they thought, as a man of wealth and power, ruling over all the earth, commanding attention wherever he went. The last thing they'd looked for was who he turned out to be—a servant, lowly, humble, gentle, poor, riding on donkeys and washing feet. No wonder they didn't recognize him.

But you have. You know who Jesus is. And now you're beginning to see how he wants you to live the singular life he gave you. You understand that he gave you one intentional life comprised of distinct qualities to be used for his purpose. It's heady stuff, to be sure. The third life choice we discussed at the beginning of this book involves living that purpose. We make this choice when we choose to follow Jesus' example. Like Jesus, our Messiah, we are here to serve.

Beginning today, we're going to look at all those puzzle pieces we examined in week two to see what it is God made the puzzle called you to do. What exactly is the big picture? Let's grab a tall cup of coffee and talk it over. In fact, take a look at that barista over there. See that apron she's wearing? That's a great symbol for our lesson for this week. An apron represents service. That's Life Choice 3.

Nowhere is this choice better defined than in the opening line of Day 1 in *The Purpose Driven Life*: "It's not about you."[1] It's a simple statement, but it's a truth both profound and life altering when we fully grasp it. We're not here for self-gratification or to become rich or famous. We are here to serve others and to do so passionately. If your heart is surrendered to God and you're obediently stewarding your gifts for Christ, you will care about what he cares about. He served others, and he asks us to do the same.

This direction comes from the lips of Jesus himself, who told his disciples, "If you try to hang on to your life, you will lose it. But if you give up your life for my sake, you will save it" (Matthew 16:25 NLT). When he made that statement, Jesus had mastered full surrender, preached parables about stewardship, and was en route to completing Life Choice 3. It was his reason for living, and it meant making the ultimate sacrifice—that of completely laying down his life on behalf of others.

I'm not saying that God is asking you to literally do what Jesus did. But, by becoming a man and living in human form, Jesus related himself to our condition. He understands, better than anyone, just how hard it is for us to give and to love sacrificially. He also comprehends, as no one else can, the glory that awaits us when we choose that kind of life.

There is no greater love
than to lay down one's life for one's friends.
John 15:13 NLT

Serving others passionately actually means giving your life away. God wants you to live beyond yourself, for only there will you find true meaning in life.

Choosing to Serve

It doesn't take an expert on history or global affairs to see that the world is full of selfish, often tyrannical leaders. Always has been. But Jesus said, "Among you it will be different. Those who are the greatest among you should take the lowest rank, and the leader should be like a servant" (Luke 22:26 NLT).

How can you use your uniqueness to lead like Jesus did? You begin by going out and looking for those people God has put in your life to lead and to love. What does sacrificial love and service look like on a daily basis? As parents, for example, we love sacrificially, putting on the servant's apron, so to speak, when we choose to love our children even when they behave in unlovely ways—and what child does not offer us that opportunity from time to time? Or we can choose to enter the workplace with a servant's attitude, ready to put on the apron and do what is needed to help our coworkers reach their goals, even if—especially if—we are the boss.

Sacrificial love is as simple as holding the door open for someone or smiling and speaking graciously even when others are gruff. It's as difficult as choosing not to turn the channel when the images of starving children in Africa make us uncomfortable, or walking by the homeless person in need of a meal instead of crossing to the other side of the street. It's as painful as saying, "I'm sorry," "Forgive me," or, "Let's try again."

Paul reminds us of how it should be with us: "You have taken off your old self with its practices and have put on the new self, which is being renewed in knowledge in the image of its Creator" (Colossians 3:9–10). We are to learn to be like Christ by behaving in a Christlike way.

What God's asking us to do is develop a servant's heart. He wants us to be centered on others rather than be stuck on self. It's a totally countercultural concept, but God has always been out of step with what's popular.

In his book *Lead Like Jesus,* business guru and author of *The One Minute Manager* Ken Blanchard helps us to see that Jesus doesn't want to be a part of our lives—he wants to be the center. Everything we do should emanate from this axis. What we believe, who we are, how we treat others, why we do what we do and when we do it—it all should flow from the Spirit of Christ in us. "Christians have more in Jesus than just a great spiritual leader," Blanchard has said. "We have a practical and effective leadership model for all organizations, for all people, for all situations. The more I read the Bible, the more I realized that Jesus did everything I ever taught or wrote about over the years and He did it perfectly. He is simply the greatest leadership model for all time."[2]

In his book Blanchard wrote, "Leadership is a process of influence. Anytime you seek to influence the thinking, behavior, or development of people toward accomplishing a goal in their personal or professional lives, you are taking on the role of a leader."[3] Maybe you've never thought of yourself as a leader before, but now that you think about it in terms of Blanchard's definition—could it be true of you? Each one of us influences others, whether we're aware of it or not. Paul told the church at Corinth, "We are therefore Christ's ambassadors, as though God were making his appeal through us. We implore you on Christ's behalf: Be reconciled to God" (2 Corinthians 5:20). Ambassadors represent a country or a king to the world. We are called to represent our King, and that means using our influence well.

So how do you learn to be a servant leader? You do it by modeling Christ in your world. You take out all those pieces in your box and use them together to love others unconditionally. Why do we do this? Scripture tells us, "We love because he first loved us" (1 John 4:19).

We may choose to serve others through our occupation or through a mission opportunity, as a young woman named Christy has. One Christmas, rather than be with her family and friends in America, Christy chose to share her life with orphans in Rwanda. "I thought, *One Christmas away from a family is bearable, but what if I were a teenage orphan and it was my tenth or eleventh separated from a family, how would I feel?* I plan on giving out a lot of hugs this year and offering a little of my time to love those who may have been overlooked in years gone by."

Christy admitted that it isn't easy to live in a land where she doesn't speak the language. "Fortunately, though, a Rwandan family has taken me under their wing and made me feel welcome, so I will learn from them the local customs and traditions for Christmas. Despite a thick language barrier between me and my new friends here, the idea that we care for one another is translated through God's grace, and I'm thankful for that."

Instead of roast turkey and pumpkin pie, Christy ate banana soup, goat brochette, and other unusual dishes. Not only has she survived, she has chosen to go on other mission adventures, sharing the love of Christ unconditionally in a land that is not her native home.

"I've come to realize that it's through the difficult times in life that God loves to shape us into something we never thought we could be," she said. "Whether we've had or have broken relationships, broken bodies, or broken pocketbooks, he somehow always manages to reach down, scoop us up, and say, 'Remember, I care for you, despite what you've done or where you've been. I care about where you are going, and you are important to me. Your life is not by chance. I have plans for you, just wait and see.'"

Christy is experiencing the love of God in ways she never could have dreamed because she has dared to put on the apron and serve people in a faraway land with unknown customs and language, showing through her service the sacrificial love of Christ.

Being Prepared

Opportunities to love unconditionally may be chosen in advance, like Christy's, or they may be thrust upon us without warning. How do we handle those moments we didn't anticipate? We get through them by being prepared in advance, by practicing the lifestyle of a servant.

During a luncheon with friends from church, Marge took a moment to freshen up in the restaurant's women's lounge. Emerging from a stall, she was confronted by a man. *What's he doing in here?* she thought. Her heart thumped and her mind raced with the possibilities. It didn't take long, however, for her to comprehend what he had in mind. As he attempted to rape her, her training kicked in. She began to tell him about Jesus. "He loves you too much to let you do this," she explained.

This was not what the man had expected, and he could not go through with the act. He collapsed and began to sob. Marge called the restaurant manager, who notified the police, but as they cuffed her assailant, Marge urged them to have mercy. Over the next weeks and months, she visited him in jail and continued to tell him about her Lord. Marge could do this because she had prepared her heart in advance by deciding to love as Jesus loved: unconditionally. In her moment of terror, she identified with the Man whose life had been given for her sake. She knew he had also died for the sake of this lost would-be rapist. And in time, that man accepted Christ into his heart.

Whenever we minister to the deepest needs of others, we offer them God's unconditional love. That person may be an orphan in Rwanda, a criminal intent on doing us harm, a homeless man in need of a meal, or your best friend whose husband was just laid off. It's not the extent of our service that matters; it's that we constantly prepare to act at Christ's urging at a moment's notice.

Action springs not from thought,
but from a readiness for responsibility.
—Dietrich Bonhoeffer

Making It Count

During his brief life on earth, Jesus served wherever he went. From the wedding at Cana, where he served by turning water into wine (John 2:1–11), to casting out demons (Matthew 8:28–34), to the healing of a man born blind (John 9:1–12), to his final act on the cross as he gave his life to break the power of sin, Jesus daily laid down his life to serve others.

God is not asking you to wear sandals and a robe or to walk with a cross over your shoulder or even to grow your hair long and go around looking pious. What he wants is your partnership. He wants you to take all the pieces he has packed inside you and use them to go out and serve others by being the you he has made you to be. That you, believe it or not, is someone who can love others unconditionally.

"But that can't be me! I don't even like my sister. How can I possibly love anyone unconditionally?" You do it by loving Jesus and then allowing yourself to be his channel to love others. It's that surrender we talked about earlier. No one said it would be easy. We are not Jesus, but we are called to be his hands and feet in this world.

Dear friends, we should love each other,
because love comes from God.
Everyone who loves has become God's child
and knows God. Whoever does not love
does not know God, because God is love.
This is how God showed his love to us:
He sent his one and only Son into the world
so that we could have life through him.
This is what real love is: It is not our love
for God; it is God's love for us.

1 John 4:7–10 NCV

We are to "think and act like Christ Jesus. Christ himself was like God in everything. But he did not think that being equal with God was something to be used for his own benefit. But he gave up his place with God and made himself nothing. He was born as a man and became like a servant" (Philippians 2:5–7 NCV).

We are imperfect people learning to be like Christ. If it were easy, no learning would be required.

To be a servant, Jesus had to take on the mind of a servant. That means accepting whatever God hands you as the task he needs you to complete for him. Martin Luther King Jr. called it "our contribution and calling," and we're to do it in a way that brings God glory and pleasure.

What is your "contribution and calling"? Is it a job you're supposed to do, a person you're meant to befriend, a need you're intended to meet, a ministry effort you're called to support financially? How does God want you to serve him by serving others? Over the next few days, we'll look more closely at how, specifically, to serve God by serving others.

Today, imagine yourself with that barista apron on—one that says something like, "Jesus Christ & Company: Millions Served Daily. How can you serve Jesus to others today? Who needs to know your uniquely blended flavor of his rich brew? Use the space below to journal the ideas he is bringing into your mind.

Let's offer up this prayer together.

Lord, I confess that I haven't thought of myself up to now as anyone's servant. In fact, there's something about that word that tends to rub me the wrong way at first. But when I think about the fact that you came as a servant, I see the word in a different light. You gave it honor and distinction. Because of your example, I long to live as a servant. Please show me how and help me to fulfill the unique reason I am here on earth. When I think of the word apron, *let me see in my mind a carpenter's apron—and help me to see that the carpenter is you.*

Now that we've put on our aprons and we're ready to serve others for Christ, tomorrow we're going to step out of our personal spaces and start looking for the people around us whom he wants us to serve—beginning with the people who live in the hallways of our lives.

Day 16

HALLWAYS

Opening Our Doors to Help Our Neighbors

*Those of us who are strong and able in the faith need to step
in and lend a hand to those who falter, and not just do what is
most convenient for us. Strength is for service, not status.
Each one of us needs to look after the good of the people around
us, asking ourselves, "How can I help?" That's exactly what
Jesus did. He didn't make it easy for himself by avoiding
people's troubles, but waded right in and helped out.
"I took on the troubles of the troubled," is the way Scripture
puts it. Even if it was written in Scripture long ago,
you can be sure it's written for us.*
Romans 15:1–4 MSG

*If my heart is right with God,
every human being is my neighbor.*
—Oswald Chambers

WHEN NEW YORK CITY Police went to investigate the murder
of a young woman stabbed to death at a nice, quiet Queens
apartment complex in August 2008, bloody handprints on the doors
in one hallway bore mute witness to a most unneighborly breach of

trust. Stabbed twelve times by an ex-boyfriend, the young mother called repeatedly for help—but no one came to help her, or even called the police. "She was screaming, 'Help, help, he stabbed me on the neck, I'm bleeding from the neck!'" a neighbor would later tell the *New York Daily News*—after not raising a finger to help that night. One neighbor told police that she had assumed the woman was drunk. Another's excuse was that he had heard cries but didn't understand English. Others insisted that they had never heard anything. No one lifted a finger to help the woman for more than thirty minutes while she desperately cried for help. "If you hear somebody screaming for their life, why would you ignore it?" the victim's sister asked, anguished, as she tried to come to grips with what had happened. "They could have helped her, they could have called the cops—she would still be with us."

Think you would have helped? I hope so. God willing, most of us will never be in a situation where we'll have to find out how we'd react in such a violent, life-or-death situation.

But how do we react every day to the cries for help of the "neighbors" who do cross our paths—the coworker who's desperately lonely; the struggling single parent whose child was just diagnosed with autism; the overweight teenager who feels unattractive and worthless; the college student who feels like a failure; the overwhelmed husband who feels like running away; the new person at church who doesn't have a clue how to break in to a group of friends; the woman starving for a word of affirmation or appreciation from someone . . . the discontented, the fearful, the grieving, the bored, the questioning, the depressed, the guilt-ridden, the wounded, the numb . . . the people you encountered even today?

Jesus calls us to love our neighbors—to open our doors rather than lock them tightly against people's needs and what it might demand of us to meet them. Are there bloody handprints on the doors of our hearts? How many neighbors have knocked, desperate for our help? What were the excuses we used for shutting our ears and our doors and hoping they'd just go away?

Hall Monitor: Who Is My Neighbor?

Few people would say that we don't have a responsibility to help our neighbors. But we have a lot of responsibilities and commitments. Just how much time and effort is this going to take? And exactly how far does our responsibility go? The houses on either side of us and right across the street, sure. Three doors down? Maybe. The next street over? The next block? The gal in the next cubicle? Just who, exactly, is our neighbor?

One day an expert in the law asked Jesus the same question. When Jesus had told the man to love God with all his heart, mind, strength, and soul and to love his neighbor as himself, the man sought to justify his actions (or lack of actions). So he asked Jesus, "Who is my neighbor?" (Luke 10:29).

Jesus told the story we're all familiar with: the story of the Good Samaritan. But really think about what Jesus was teaching through this story. A man was traveling along the road, maybe on his way to a business meeting, when a group of muggers jumped him, beat him, and robbed him, leaving him for dead by the side of the road. A priest walking by saw him lying there—and quickly crossed to the other side of the road. Some time later another man, a member of a priestly family, walked by, saw the guy, and did the same thing. They couldn't get away fast enough.

During those days there was a group of people called Samaritans (people from Samaria), whom the Jews looked down upon. So Jesus, fully aware of what the Hebrew legal eagle in front of him thought about people from Samaria, told about a Samaritan man who came along, saw the injured man, had compassion on him, and chose to help him out. He took him to a place where he would be safe and could rest as he healed, left enough money to pay for his immediate needs, promising to pay more when he returned if that was needed, and went on his way.

Jesus asked the law specialist, "Which of these three do you think was a neighbor to the man who fell into the hands of robbers?" (Luke 10:36). Scripture doesn't tell us whether the man squirmed as he answered, but he said, "The one who had mercy on him." Jesus told the man, "Go and do likewise" (Luke 10:37).

I know it sounds hard to believe, in our era of gridlocked highways and soaring gas prices, but years ago, people got where they were going on foot. This is how it was when Jesus walked the earth . . . and walked and walked and walked. So when he told the story of the Good Samaritan, his listeners could relate to seeing someone hurt on the side of the road and in need of help. Today we zoom right past people who have car trouble. After all, they can just call AAA on their cell phones, right? But in Jesus' day, people relied on help from one another much more than we do today.

As for traveling on foot, most of the walking we do is down hallways—office hallways, the hallways of our homes, or up and down hallways in the mall. It's not likely we're going to come across people in our day-to-day dealings who've been beaten and robbed, but the point is more about the answer to the question, "Who is my neighbor?" It's not necessarily the family next door or even the people in your neighborhood, though those folks are definitely neighbors. Jesus wants you to expand your worldview. Remember that in Jesus' day, the number of people you likely had contact with in your whole life was relatively few compared with how many we can touch in some way every day today. Technological improvements like cell phones, email, and air travel have opened up whole new possibilities for defining *neighbor*. Who are the people in your hallways? How can you use those special ingredients that God used to make you to show them Jesus today?

Hall Duty: When Opportunity Knocks

No one has ever seen God,
but if we love each other, God lives in us,
and his love is made perfect in us.
1 John 4:12 NCV

Are you waiting for opportunity to knock? It's already knocking. Open the door and you'll find . . . your neighbor, a person God has sent your way to love and serve as you point him or her to Christ. You'll find many such people in the hallways of your life every day and every week—service people at stores and restaurants, the mail carrier, your coworker, the man who walks his dog past your house every day, the women at the hair salon, your dentist, your son's teacher, the political worker canvassing your neighborhood—even the telemarketer who interrupts your dinner. They are your neighbors.

God wants us to expand our hearts by learning to love as Jesus loved. To do that, we need to open our eyes and see the people and needs around us.

In his book *Living a Life on Loan: Finding Grace at the Intersections,* Rick Rusaw writes:

> I don't really remember much from driver's ed class, except one thing that instructor kept repeating. That one thing has stuck with me all these years and still influences the way I drive today. "Always watch out for the intersections, Rick. Good things and bad things can happen at intersections."
>
> That's exactly God's message to you: pay attention at the intersections. Keep your eyes open and look at what might be going on when you cross paths with another person."[1]

This is how being a good neighbor works, too. We pay attention whenever God brings another person into our lives. What does he have in mind for this encounter, however brief, or for this relationship? How can we maximize our service for God by paying attention at this intersection?

You may be climbing the ladder to the top of your corporation, or you may be the quietest sheep in the flock. No matter what your daily role, if you influence someone else's life in any way, you have the opportunity to serve God by serving others. Whether you're a boss, a mom, a fast-food counter clerk, or the shortstop on your baseball team—

somebody out there is watching you, and God has put you in this person's life so that he or she can see what Jesus looks like. You might even be the only representative of Jesus that person will ever meet.

"But I can't love those people," you may protest. "I don't even like most people!" God never said it would be easy. But I invite you to consider that God has placed you in a community, hallways full of people who need to be loved as only you can love them.

Part of God's purpose in your life is to make you more like Jesus. So what did Jesus do when he needed help? He turned to the Father. Follow his example. When a person in your life seems impossible to love, ask God to love that person through you. Then act like you love him or her, and watch God bring the feelings along as a consequence of your obedience. I love how he does that.

It won't always be easy. It'll seldom be convenient. But don't let that derail your efforts to be a good neighbor. A review of Jesus' life on earth reveals that his most notable acts of healing were done at times when it was inconvenient. He was frequently interrupted by others. But no matter what he was doing or where he was going, Jesus allowed himself to be stopped, his attention diverted, his energies invested at a moment's notice. He recognized that his path was laid out by God's design and with God's permission. Every day and every minute were at the Father's disposal.

The Hall Effect: The Door Swings Both Ways

"I sure could use a good neighbor myself," you might say. "So how can I minister to others when I so need someone to minister to me?"

Let me tell you about my friend Louise. When Louise became disabled, her son reluctantly realized that she would be best cared for in an assisted-living facility. Louise was so unhappy about this arrangement that at first she refused to get to know her new neighbors. The only time she went out at all was on Sundays, when a shuttle bus came to take residents to church.

One Sunday she prayed, "Lord, help me. I'm in trouble!" Then she read in the church bulletin about small groups forming for Bible study and fellowship. "Is that you, Lord?" Louise asked when she felt her heart leap. That week she began traveling the hallways in her new home, inviting her neighbors to join her in Bible study. Before long that group became the answer to each member's prayers. So Louise's trouble became a way to help those around her. Louise became a good neighbor—a Good Samaritan—and in the process, she helped herself, too. Her own needs for fellowship and help through a difficult transition were met by the very people whose needs she met. That's how it always seems to work with God. The greatest blessing always is ours when we seek to bless others.

The truth is that we need other people. We're better when we work together and support one another. If you're a fan of C. S. Lewis and J. R. R. Tolkien, you may have read about their writers' group, known as the Inklings. Back in the 1930s and '40s, they met regularly and read one another's works in progress. You can imagine how tough that crowd was. Over the years, these men became so instrumental in one another's lives that one author argues that beloved works such as *The Chronicles of Narnia* and *The Lord of the Rings* might never have been published, or at least not in the form we know them today, had it not been for the Inklings.[2] What's more, without the influence of Tolkien and other believing members of the Inklings, C. S. Lewis may never have become the Christian that God meant for him to be. What a tragic loss that would have been. The Bible tells us that "as iron sharpens iron, so one man sharpens another" (Proverbs 27:17). As the Inklings' writings were improved by their collective encouragement, so God designed us to be sharpened and strengthened by living and serving in community.

There really is no situation in which God can't use you to be a Good Samaritan to some neighbor he has brought into your life. Who lives in your hallways?

> Speak encouraging words to one another.
> Build up hope so you'll all be together in this,
> no one left out, no one left behind.
> I know you're already doing this;
> just keep on doing it.
> 1 Thessalonians 5:11 MSG

Something in us often finds it difficult to fit into groups—or even to think we need them. We'll spend years and great energy seeking out a life mate, but when it comes to a group of friends . . . well, we think we can get along on our own. But God never meant us to live that way. After all, what good are all those puzzle pieces if no one ever sees the completed puzzle? What good are all those ingredients if no one ever experiences your unique flavor?

The Bible tells us, "Our bodies have many parts, and God has put each part just where he wants it" (1 Corinthians 12:18 NLT). You need the body of Christ, and the body of Christ needs you.

Making It Count

So how good a neighbor are you? How can you be the neighbor God wants you to be and has gifted you to be? Consider today the practical ways you can open your doors to your neighbors in need.

Are you a mom? Of course, your kids expect you to be their slave. But how would it change things if you saw yourself as serving Jesus by serving them?

Are you the barista in this coffee shop? Customer-service jobs can get to be a real grind after a while (pardon the pun). So how could it perk up your day to think of those customers, especially the crabby, demanding ones, as your mission field? I'm not suggesting you grab each one by the collar and begin preaching a salvation message—that might not go over well with the boss. What I am suggesting is that you treat them as Jesus would. Let them see what having a servant's heart looks like before they get to work and are scowled at again.

Be creative. Ask God to help you see who lives in your hallways. It may be your family, your coworkers, your classmates, the strangers who cross your path in the store or on the bus, or your actual next-door neighbors. It may even be people on the other side of the globe with whom you communicate every day by email or connect with on business trips. Each one of these people is your neighbor. How can you be a Good Samaritan in their lives? You don't need to have the answer right now. This is not a pass-or-fail exam. You just need to be open and aware and seeking. God has promised, "You will seek me and find me when you seek me with all your heart" (Jeremiah 29:13). Will you seek him wholeheartedly? It's the only way to become fully you.

As you walk through the hallways of your life today, keep your eyes open. Be alert. Who needs a helping hand that you can offer? In the space below, write down some neighborly opportunities that come to mind.

Ask God to show you whose life needs a touch from him today that can come through your servant hands. In fact, let's do that together right now.

Father, help me to be aware of the people in my hallways today and to see who needs a helping hand. Then help me not to be selfish when that request or awareness dawns on me, but let me be ready and willing to extend your love and service to my neighbor. Remind me throughout this day that the world around me needs to see you and that they can see you in me if I allow you to live in me. Please, Lord Jesus, live in me.

Tomorrow we'll look beyond the hallways of our everyday lives and see who else is out there who might need to hear the message we've been given to share. Who knows—they might even enjoy a cup of coffee now and then, too.

Day 17

TAKEOUT

Sharing Christ with the Spiritually Hungry

We cannot help speaking about what we have seen and heard.
Acts 4:20

Witnessing is not a spare-time occupation
or a once-a-week activity. It must be a quality of life.
You don't go witnessing, you are a witness.
—Dan Greene

ONE OF THE BEST things about these little coffee shops is the option they give you to drink your coffee there in the shop or to take it with you. The gospel is like that, too. The difference is that with God, it's not an either/or option but a both/and decision. He wants us to both drink deeply of his truths in the quiet of our favorite places and then take them out to the world around us.

Has God made a difference in your life? If so, you've become an eyewitness to the gospel in action. Nothing pleases God more than for you to tell your story to someone whose life needs that same difference—the change only he can bring.

Taking our faith out into the world is our most important job for God, but, oddly enough, it's also the one area where we're likely to find the most resistance—and most of that comes from within ourselves. Why don't we share our faith more often? Mostly it's because we are afraid—afraid of being rejected or of having others think we're weird, or for some other reason that really has little substance if we think about it for long. Here in America, at least, no one can stop us from sharing our faith but ourselves.

Taking the Bread of Life to a Hungry World

Do you know what it feels like to be really hungry? The way we eat in America, almost as a sport or at least as a social event, some of us probably don't ever feel hungry. We eat to keep from being hungry or because something smells or looks good and tempts us to indulge.

That's sort of how it is for us spiritually when we have a personal relationship with Jesus. We feel fulfilled, satisfied, and are constantly fed spiritually at church and in our own times of Bible study and devotion. We may feel spiritual desire and longing for more of God, but it's nothing compared to the desperate, aching, empty feeling that's inside so many people around us. Some try to fill the empty space with other things—experiences, pleasures, relationships, wealth, possessions, accomplishments, fame, adventure—but the hunger can never be satisfied for long. Only Christ truly satisfies that deep-down spiritual hunger. "Jesus declared, 'I am the bread of life. He who comes to me will never go hungry, and he who believes in me will never be thirsty'" (John 6:35).

God wants us to share the "bread of life" with those around us. But sometimes we shy away from taking the lead in talking with our friends and coworkers about important spiritual matters. We don't want to impose on them or make them uncomfortable. What if we wouldn't have all the right answers? What if they think we're foolish or intolerant? What if it changes everything between us? Or we assume they wouldn't be interested: after all, they seem to be doing okay as they are.

We forget about the God-shaped hole, the spiritual hunger, that

God has placed in every person's soul—the part that feels something is missing until fellowship with God is restored. All we must do is be faithful when God opens doors of opportunity to speak about him— just to tell what we know, have seen, and have experienced in our lives. How tough is that? We're like the delivery driver: Jesus is the bread of life, and the Holy Spirit is the tantalizing aroma that draws people to him.

> You are to be his witness, telling everyone
> what you have seen and heard.
> Acts 22:15 NLT

Following are a couple of examples of ordinary guys who were faithful to carry out Christ's mission by sharing their spiritual experiences with others.

Jeff's Take-home

While playing golf one day with his friend Chris, Jeff sensed the Holy Spirit prompting him to go deeper. Chris had let his questions and doubts keep him from crossing the line into a full-on relationship with Jesus. Uncomfortable with opening up on the golf course, Jeff invited Chris and his wife to his home, hoping for an opportunity to discuss those questions. God blessed that invitation, and in time Chris abandoned his doubt by inviting Jesus into his heart.

"It was great for me to see this process," Jeff said. "If you really get to know people and you let them see who you are and you've showed that you care, then you have the credibility to bring up spiritual issues. People really want to talk about these issues. The rejection and the fear were my own problems—they weren't reality."[1]

Dave's Delivery

Following a terrible motorcycle accident, Dave needed a transfusion to keep him alive. Ten years would pass before he learned that the blood he'd been given was tainted with the HIV virus. Dave and his wife, Kim, were devastated. And then they were shunned. They lost friends, jobs, and even their church.

When Dave realized how badly he had let this dilemma shake his faith, he surrendered his life to God afresh. The new church Dave and his wife had been attending was recruiting people to go on mission trips, and Dave surprised himself by approaching the pastor. "Hi, I'm Dave Storm," he heard himself say, "and I have AIDS. I'd like to go to Africa."

Dave told the pastor what his medical needs would be during such a trip, knowing that might disqualify him. But the pastor pledged to get him what he needed. Because Dave and Kim allowed God to work through the unique circumstances of their lives, today God is using their pain to deliver badly needed hope to people around the world suffering from HIV/AIDS.[2]

The Takeaway

Jeff related to Chris because he'd been where Chris was. Dave could relate to people in Africa suffering from HIV/AIDS because he suffers from it. God has put people in your life who need to hear what you've been through, too. Your personality attracts others to you so that you can share your experiences in a way that resonates with their own. I don't know exactly how this works, but I've seen God do it over and over again—so I know it works. My guess is that at some time and in some way, you related to something someone was going through and were able to encourage him or her by sharing your story. You never know how God might want to use you to serve those in need. Your mission is to be open and available to him, ready to speak about what you know and have experienced in Christ.

More Than Words

To be a witness does not consist of engaging
in propaganda or in stirring people up.
It means to live in such a way that one's life
would not make sense if God did not exist.
—Emmanuel Suhard

Sharing the bread of life with those around us is not strictly a verbal exercise. More often than not, our actions speak louder than our words. Our lives are constantly shouting out messages to others: either positive messages of Christ's love for them or negative messages that will sour people on us and, maybe, our God. We choose the positive message when we build relationships with people and allow them to see God in us.

One way to begin building relationships with others is through meeting a need in their lives. If you come empty-handed and just start spouting scriptures, you're likely wasting your breath. But once you've met a person's deepest needs, he or she will listen to what you have to say. Following are some examples of ordinary believers who earned the right to speak for Christ by their loving actions.

Calling for Take-out: Faith That Leads to Works

When God blesses us, it's not so that we can hold up our stuff and say, "See?" He wants us to use what he's given us to bless others. Faith demonstrates itself in action. Both Paul and James tell us this. Paul wants us to know it's the reason we were saved: "God saved you by his grace when you believed. And you can't take credit for this; it is a gift from God. Salvation is not a reward for the good things we have done, so none of us can boast about it. For we are God's masterpiece. He has created us anew in Christ Jesus, so we can do the good things he planned for us long ago" (Ephesians 2:8–10 NLT). We are saved to do good things.

James takes this argument a step further by stating, "Faith by itself isn't enough. Unless it produces good deeds, it is dead and useless" (James 2:17 NLT).

Is there a dream, a desire, a wish for others that God has put in your heart? Maybe this is where your faith is meant to take action.

Joy and Jeff's faith led to one good deed that changed someone's life forever. They already had four kids and a list of ministries in which they were involved. Really, it was enough. That weekend they'd heard a couple in church share about stepping out in faith to adopt an orphan from China. For some reason, they couldn't shake it off. "I challenge you," the pastor had said, "to take to God your excuses for not serving people in need. Ask him to tell you whether they are legitimate." Excuses? Joy and Jeff had legitimate reasons!

"That night, Joy and I decided to take an honest look at the roadblocks that would prevent us from stepping out in faith," Jeff said. "There were many! So we prayed. Not long after that, we met a family who had just adopted two boys from Africa. They knew about two other little boys in a Kenyan orphanage. What a great opportunity it would be for us, they said. Whoa—were we ready for this? We talked it over with our kids and were surprised at how supportive they were, volunteering to give up things in their lives in order to help save money. Our hearts were touched by their generosity. We realized we had no excuses. This was about God's glory, not our ability or comfort."

New Orleans Po-boys: Bridges Built in Disaster

In the aftermath of Hurricane Katrina in 2005, it became clear to many who came to the aid of those impacted that only the church is big enough to handle disasters of this magnitude. While the media focused on 18,000 people being housed at the Houston Astrodome, local churches were caring for more than 150,000.

One group from Celebration Church in New Orleans saw a woman crying over the loss of her home, a single mother desperate to put a roof over her family's heads. While one church member took her to lunch and shopping for clothes, the rest of the group began working on her house. Sobbing for joy at what she saw when she returned, the woman asked, "How could anyone love me that much?" What an opportunity that group had to lead this woman to the Lord.[3]

Disaster presents us with unique and unprecedented opportunities to mobilize the hands and feet of the body of Christ. But we don't need to wait for tragedy to strike. People around us have needs every day that we can meet. We must ask God to open our eyes, and we must be ready.

What has God given you that you can use to help someone? I'm not talking about handouts, but it's amazing what can be accomplished when we're willing to lend someone a hand up and out of trouble.

Global Franchise: The P.E.A.C.E. Plan

In 2003 my pastor, Rick Warren, launched what I believe is the most audacious plan in recent church history. He calls it the P.E.A.C.E. Plan, and its goal is to eradicate what Rick has identified as the five global giants: (1) spiritual darkness; (2) a lack of servant leaders; (3) poverty; (4) disease; and (5) ignorance. By equipping local churches throughout the world, the plan aims to topple these giants using a five-pronged approach: (1) **P**romoting reconciliation; (2) **E**quipping servant leaders; (3) **A**ssisting the poor; (4) **C**aring for the sick; and (5) **E**ducating the next generation (hence the anagram P.E.A.C.E.). As with any new endeavor, it has been finding its legs gradually, but there is no doubt that the P.E.A.C.E. Plan is moving steadily and mightily forward. Thousands of people around the world have and are participating. Anyone can take part in any number of ways, from taking a mission trip to donating money to praying for this plan. (If you'd like to learn more, visit http://www .thepeaceplan.com.) It's amazing what's being accomplished—and what remains to be done—by what Rick calls "ordinary people empowered by God making a difference together wherever they are."[4]

Like Jeff and Joy, like the church members who went to New Orleans, and like all those taking part in the P.E.A.C.E. Plan, you have been blessed in order to be a blessing. How does God want to use you to meet a need in his name? Is there a place you could volunteer in your community to serve people in need? What about using all God has given you to serve people overseas? Take a step of faith and serve someone this week. Meet a need. Fill a hole. Act in kindness. Make your life a living testimony to the love and transforming power of God. Make people hungry for more of God in their lives.

Making It Count

A story on the Internet tells of a boy who wanted to go to see God. Knowing it would be a long trip, he packed his suitcase with Twinkies and root beer. After traveling a few blocks, he came upon an elderly man feeding pigeons in the park.

Needing a break from his journey, the boy sat down on the bench near the man and opened his suitcase for a little refreshment. That's when he noticed that the man looked hungry. He offered him a Twinkie, and the man gratefully accepted it, smiling. The little boy loved the smile and wanted to see it again, so he offered the man a root beer. He was not disappointed. They sat there all afternoon, neither of them speaking a word but thoroughly enjoying each other's company.

As it grew dark, the boy realized that he needed to go home. He took a few steps and then, turning around, he ran back to give the man a big hug. He'd never seen a bigger smile.

When he got home, his mom asked him what he'd been doing that made him so happy. The boy answered, "I had lunch with God today. He's got the best smile I've ever seen."

Meanwhile, at the elderly man's home, his son asked, "What's made you so happy?" The old man replied, "I met God today. You know, he's much younger than I expected."

We never know who needs to see God in our lives. Who knows how many people we meet each day who have hunger that only God can fill. But we can know that God will use us in amazing ways if we simply ask expectantly and stand ready to serve as he directs.

One of the best ways to get ready to share God's love is to write your story. How has God made a difference in your life? When has he met you in a way that changed you forever or delivered you from an "impossible" circumstance?

Take a few minutes today and write that story. Call it your eyewitness testimony, and let God use it as the evidence that someone needs in order to believe. When you meet someone new, ask that person to share his or her story, too. It's a great way to get to know each other and to find that common ground, the place where you can take out the truths God has given you and share them with another who needs to hear them.

Look for occasions to bless others with your actions or your words. It can be as simple as roaming your hallways in search of those who are hurting or checking in with your church to discover serving opportunities in your community.

You may hear the phrase *on mission* and think of it as applying only to those who choose to serve as missionaries. But as believers we are all called to be "on mission" each and every day. We're to feast on God's truths—and then to take them out to a world that is starving for them.

Let's ask God to help us do that.

Father, help me to be someone who's ready to offer your bread of life to the spiritually hungry. Give me eyes to see them, a heart to love them, hands to help them, and your words to feed them. Whether or not I am ever sent out on a mission trip, help me to see myself as "on mission" for you every day and in every place you put me. Thank you for helping me to understand this essential purpose of my life.

Tomorrow we'll explore how to find our special ministry fit at church. Meet you back here . . . where, by now, we know the coffee is always just the way we like it.

DOES THE BODY GOOD

Finding Your Fit

Just as each of us has one body with many members,
and these members do not all have the same function,
so in Christ we who are many form one body,
and each member belongs to all the others.
Romans 12:4–5

Individual commitment to a group effort—that is what makes a
team work, a company work, a society work, a civilization work.
—Vince Lombardi

HAVE YOU EVER HAD a pair of shoes that didn't quite fit at first? You wear them for a few hours, and pretty soon there's a tenderness where your heel meets the stiff back of the shoe. That's when you realize that your first mistake was wearing them to Disneyland and not bringing a spare pair. Before you know it, you've got giant blisters on your feet. Your initial excitement over the new shoes is gone, and now you just can't wait to get them off. Bring on the Band-Aids!

Figuring out how we fit in at church can feel that way sometimes—like everything we try just raises big, painful blisters. It's enough to keep some people from trying to fit at all. After all, who needs more irritation, especially with the emotional blisters life already brings our way?

But the apostle Paul has made it clear that we're meant to be moving, usable parts of this body of Christ we find ourselves in. It's one thing to realize how God designed us and wants to use us individually, but how can we find out where we fit in this body that often rubs us the wrong way?

Maybe you're still trying to find the perfect pastor, the right church, or the best small group. My suggestion to you is that you stop *trying* and start *being*. We've all had painful experiences with others, but God didn't put us here to live isolated, "me first" lives.

One thing I realized long ago is that what God tells us to do is seldom easy. If it were, we'd do it without being told to. So he says, "Love your neighbor as yourself," because it's hard to do and few of us would do it on our own. Getting along with others is the first hurdle we must cross before we can find where and how we fit. This requires letting Jesus love other people through us, as we've been discussing this week. It's as true at church as anywhere else in this world.

As Christians we should be more like Christ, but the fact is that we're still just imperfect people. If you can accept that fact and move past the imperfections and into service within the body, you'll be on your way to a process that promises to refine your uniqueness, refresh your spirit, and refocus your life like nothing else can: finding your fit at church.

You First

Your church is one of the best places to discover the you that only you can be. Do you see a place where you'd like to serve or a need that's not being met? This might be precisely where God wants you to serve in ministry. Over time, God may even raise you to lead a ministry and fully develop your unique abilities, gifts, and passions through serving God and others. That's how it worked for Helen.

By age thirty-five Helen had reached the top of the corporate ladder. Her childhood dream to run a company had come true. She was successful and well respected: life was good. But God was beginning to work in her heart, revealing a vision that would slowly unfold over the next several years. "I had what I wanted, but something was missing," she said. "It wasn't so much that it wasn't enough, but, I realize now, God had already begun blowing cold air on the hot coals of my dream. He showed me that I'd spent the first forty years of my life living for myself. On my fortieth birthday, I told him, 'I am declaring that I'll live the next forty years as the apostles.'" She realized her need to live for Christ, as a disciple who was unafraid to go wherever he sent her in order to deliver his message. What that would mean where her big corporate job was concerned, she had no idea; but for the first time, she realized, someone else was in charge.

And then one day it all came crashing down. "After managing a multimillion-dollar budget for a Fortune 500 company, my job was just—gone," Helen recalled. Yet through her pain, heartache, and loss, she discovered the power of a surrendered life.

As the months passed after her layoff, Helen got involved in developing a ministry at her church to help people practically apply their faith in the workplace. "All of my education, training, experience, and mentoring had been geared toward achieving my goals and dreams in the business world," Helen said. "But in this wilderness it seemed that God had closed those doors to my life—areas in which he had previously granted me much success. So on my knees and through tears and grief of loss, I told God I understood I was not to go back into the workplace as I had planned, and that I willingly gave up my hopes, dreams, and ambitions for which I had worked all my life. 'Lord,' I said, 'I accept whatever you have planned, but give me new hopes and dreams.'

"One day it occurred to me that the only work in my life that God was blessing was my ministry. That's when he brought me to a place of finally saying, 'If only one person's life is changed as a result of what I'm doing here, it's enough.' Then a pastor told me about a woman who'd said that if she hadn't met me, she never would have known she could have a relationship with Christ, never known her work had significance, and never realized the eternal connection between her work and God's kingdom. That was my one person. Since then, God has used our workplace ministry to change hundreds of lives and is definitely stirring up change in the local workplace." Since God put Helen in this role, small workplace groups have been mushrooming in her community as a direct result of her efforts.

Because she was determined to know what God was doing in her life and why, because she willingly surrendered her life, her abilities, her work, and her future, Helen is now living a life fully powered by God. When she was offered a staff position at her church, she said, "It was as if I heard him say to me, 'That's why you're there.' I finally got it."

God is using Helen's gifts, her abilities, her experiences, her passion, and her on-fire personality to change the lives of those around her. "I still love business," Helen explained, "but God has put such a love and burning in my heart that I'm willing to do whatever it takes so someone else can know the freedom I have." This is the kind of joy God wants you to know in serving others, and it comes from discovering the you that only you can be—so that you can do what God created you—and only you—to do.

Ephesians 2:8–10 tells us that we are saved specifically to do good works. Those works do not save us—God alone holds that key: "It is by grace you have been saved, through faith—and this not from yourselves, it is the gift of God—not by works, so that no one can boast," Paul wrote (Ephesians 2:8–9). He finished that thought by explaining why we are saved: "For we are God's workmanship, created in Christ Jesus to do good works, which God prepared in advance for us to do" (Ephesians 2:10). It's through our service in the body of Christ that we discover what God has prepared in advance for us to do—and that we do those good works.

The church is intended to be Christ's body at work in this world, bringing hope and healing to others while we are here and training up the next generation to pick up where we will leave off one day. We do that best through serving in ministries at our churches. So, how can you find your fit without too many blisters? Forgive me if I'm repeating myself, but the best way—the way I've both tried and tested—is through trying on a lot of ministries.

That brings me back to one of my earlier questions: do you belong to a local church? If not, you really do need to find one. Don't expect to find a perfect one—perfect churches don't exist. But look for one that is growing and serving the community. That's where you're likely to find your place to shine.

Trying Things on for Size

Through serving in ministry, you can fully explore your uniqueness. Here's how it works: when you went into that shoe store, you had to try on a few pairs before you found one you liked and that fit. Even then, when you started wearing them for more than a few minutes at the store, they may have rubbed a bit while you got used to them. In finding your ministry fit, you'll have to try a few on for size to see what fits—and even then you can expect a little friction now and then.

You love kids, so you work in the nursery. It's a great day—almost. The babies were cute and bubbly, until one of them bubbled all down the front of your new shirt. Does a spot on your shirt mean that ministry isn't for you? Of course not. It just means there may be a little more work and inconvenience involved than you'd realized.

You love making people feel welcome, so you decide to try the greeting ministry. It's a little awkward at first, but before you know it you've got that hand out and a smile plastered across your face that says, *Welcome! Thanks for being here today,* more convincingly than any words coming out of your mouth. Every now and then a grumpy person scowls and walks past your outstretched hand. In the beginning, that hurt a little. But then you realized that God was giving you a challenge. It might be to break through that person's tough skin with some extra kindness, or it may be that God wants you to understand his own heart a little more by seeing how he feels when people reject him. After a few weeks, you realize it's not so hard to go "out front." When a great position opens up at work that requires an extroverted personality, you ace the interview. And all because of the ministry you chose at church.

Of course, I'm painting pictures from examples I've seen over the years. It doesn't always work this harmoniously. You might try out a ministry or two—or even three or four—before you find the one that works for you and with you. It's easy to get stuck in one that isn't really where you belong. You commit to it and then realize it's not a good fit for you, but you don't know how to tell the leader. Trust me, if the ministry isn't right for you, even if the leader is initially disappointed by your decision to resign, the ministry is better off without you. Over the years I've seen that once you plug into the ministry that matches your unique design to serve, it isn't long before *you* are the leader, hearing others tell you the ministry isn't their fit. God made each of us to fit in a special place and time—or maybe even for several special places and times. Our role is to seek out where we best fit. Like Prince Charming, you might have to meet a few ugly stepsisters before you find your Cinderella ministry, where the shoe fits.

Last week we talked about the gifts God gives us for serving (page 142). Refer to that list as often as necessary to help you figure out what your ministry should be, or at least in what area you may be called to serve. Pray and ask God to give you guidance as you seek to be the you that only you can be through serving in your church. In time, you'll find freedom and fulfillment in knowing that you're serving as God designed you to serve.

Making It Count

Valerie wrote:

> Before renewing my life in Christ I was like most of the world. Proud and stiff-necked—I was out for me first. The

thought of serving another with no gain to myself was as alien as an afternoon stroll on the sun. Even when I acted like I was serving another—on the inside I was always looking for the angle. When I came back to Christ it took awhile [sic] for me to find the joy of serving another. I responded to Jesus' call to the Care Fresno Kids ministry not because I wanted to serve but because obeying His call was better than being swallowed by some fish. Over the years I have made a 180-degree change in that attitude. I love to serve. I serve Jesus first, then my family and my community of faith. People tell me that they don't understand how I do all that I do at the church. They don't know that what I am given the privilege of doing in Jesus' name isn't tiring—it is exhilarating! Life holds no greater joy than to serve in Jesus' name.[1]

Are you smelling the coffee? Serving in ministry is what you were made for! Only through serving will you find genuine life, as Valerie has, as Helen has, and as have millions of people in the church today—not to mention the billions throughout history.

You may not go to a big church with lots of options for involvement, but without a doubt, a church in your community needs your help. If you're currently plugged into a church, find out what ministries they offer. Ask for a list of ministries or a ministry brochure or a website link—something that lets you know how and where you can serve. Ask God to help you pick one to start with. Many churches have ministry fairs every year. Find out if and when your church offers one, and plan to attend. That way, you can check out what's already going on in the way of ministry and see if one or more might be your ministry dancing shoes.

Or maybe you've been wishing your church offered something that you don't see now. Guess what that means? You've got an opportunity to start and lead that ministry.

Since through God's mercy
we have this ministry, we do not lose heart!
2 Corinthians 4:1

This is the big picture: God has a place in which you are made to fit. Find it, and you'll find a way to serve with fulfillment and fruitfulness, not frustration. Be who God made you to be. When you're serving the body of Christ, you'll find refreshment for your soul and energy to go on. Like Helen, Valerie, and so many others I've met, you just might find yourself saying, "This is what I've been looking for all my life."

Will you pray with me?

Father, we recognize that you have made us for ministry, but finding that ministry often seems like trying to solve a big puzzle, and we're not sure where our pieces fit. But we trust you to show us how to become fruitful, fulfilled servants as we faithfully seek out those places you've prepared for us. Help us to be useful members of the body of Christ, for whom we are so grateful. It's in his name we pray . . . Amen.

Let's meet back here tomorrow for another cup of joe, and we'll take the idea of finding your fit in service to the next level—to discovering the joy of serving with others, of doing life together. It can sound scary at first, but you'll discover that most people are just "regular Joes" like you—and that we all need one another.

Day 19

LIFE SUPPORT

Serving with Others

All the believers lived in a wonderful harmony,
holding everything in common. They sold whatever they owned
and pooled their resources so that each person's need was met.
Acts 2:44–45 MSG

We don't accomplish anything in this world alone . . .
and whatever happens is the result of the whole tapestry
of one's life and all the weavings of individual threads
from one to another that creates something.
—Justice Sandra Day O'Connor

REMEMBER THE SCENE IN *The Lord of the Rings: The Return of the King* where Frodo and Sam—dirty, worn, and weary after weeks and months of battling villainous foes much bigger and stronger than them—finally made it to Mount Doom, where they were to throw the ring back into the fire from which it had been forged? They were so close to their goal, yet the weight of his burden was so heavy that Frodo collapsed, near death, on the mountainside. Determined and desperate, the war-weary Sam cries out, "Come on, Mr. Frodo. I can't carry it for you . . . but I can carry you!" Then he throws Frodo over his shoulder and marches resolutely forward to help him accomplish his mission—or die trying.

Whenever I watch that film or read the classic books to my kids, I think, *Wow, what a friend that Sam is. Who would do that for me?* Sam left behind his home, his family, his comfort, his safety, and even his Fellowship of the Ring friends to risk his life with Frodo in order to save Middle Earth. They knew the odds were stacked against them. They knew the chances of coming back alive were slim to none. But they did it anyway, for the Shire. And they succeeded, largely because they did it together.

There's a widely told story of a small boy feeling scared and alone in his dark bedroom late one night. He cries out to his parents in the next bedroom, "I'm scared!" His father, not wanting to get up, responds, "Don't be afraid, God is with you." After a brief pause, the little boy responds, "But, Daddy, I need someone with skin on." Even when we're all grown-up and confident that God, our Father, is with us, we still understand that little boy's feeling. God has promised that he will always be there for us: "The Lord your God goes with you; he will never leave you nor forsake you" (Deuteronomy 31:6). What's more, Jesus has called us friends: "I've named you friends because I've let you in on everything I've heard from the Father" (John 15:15 MSG). These amazing promises make my heart swell with joy. I'm grateful to know that God is always there for me—and that Jesus Christ calls me his friend! But every now and then, we all need someone with skin on.

The Bible tells us that a real friend, like Sam, sticks closer than a brother (Proverbs 18:24 NLT). So let me ask you, do you have a Samwise Gamgee in your life? Do you have anyone of whom you can say, "This is my friend who sticks closer to me than a brother"? Someone who knows you almost as well as God does? If not, let me encourage you to seek out that friend. Here's a hint: you find such a friend by being one.

Frodo found Sam in the Shire, their local community, where they lived and served together. Together they discovered the truth of Ecclesiastes 4:9–12: "Two people are better off than one, for they can help each other succeed. If one person falls, the other can reach out and help. But someone who falls alone is in real trouble. Likewise, two people lying close together can keep each other warm. But how can one be warm alone? A person standing alone can be attacked and defeated, but two can stand back-to-back and conquer. Three are even better, for a triple-braided cord is not easily broken."

Better Together

In Genesis we read that God looked on Adam and saw that it wasn't good for man to be alone. Because of this, he made Eve: "Then the LORD God said, 'It is not good for the man to be alone. I will make a helper who is just right for him'" (Genesis 2:18 NLT). Now, that was a great idea!

From our earliest moments of life, we are drawn to other people. Just watch a baby riding through a store in a shopping cart, giggling and cooing to every passerby. Watch children on the playground, magnetically drawn to one another. If even God wanted companionship, why wouldn't we? We are, after all, made in his image (Genesis 1:26–27). If just one companion had been enough for God, he would have stopped after he had created just one, Adam. Clearly, he did not. We see abundant evidence of that truth every time we get on the freeway here in Southern California, where I live. God meant for us to live, breathe, and serve with others.

Have you ever been on a team? Maybe a softball team, a drama club, or a work group? If you have, you may relate to the team Jesus built. As God, Jesus could have chosen to complete his mission alone; but he didn't. He wanted people to walk with him, to pray with him, to learn from him, and to carry on his mission after he was gone. Wherever Jesus went, people gathered. Many followed him, longing to learn from him. Finding disciples wasn't hard.

But Jesus wanted a team—a few select individuals he could pour himself into. Here's how Scripture says he gathered his team: "Jesus went up on a mountain to pray, and he prayed to God all night. At daybreak he called together all of his disciples and chose twelve of them to be apostles" (Luke 6:12–13 NLT). First, he prayed. Then he went after those people the Father had revealed to him. Finally, he put them in new places on the team. They had been disciples, but now he called them apostles. More than a disciple, Jesus' apostles were commissioned as his messengers and special representatives. They were no longer part of the crowd: they became his closest confidants—his inner circle.

At church you are one of many members, each seeking to know God better. But in ministry—that service choice we've been talking about this week—is where you really "do church". I've found serving with a team to be extremely rewarding and highly successful. Jesus set the pattern for us, showing that our effectiveness is multiplied when we are part of a team—our own inner circle with whom we can serve and grow. We can find that team by following Jesus' model of (1) asking God for wisdom and direction, (2) joining or building a team, and then (3) seeking to be placed within that team in a position where you can maximize your strengths for service.

In community we experience the love of God as people build one another up, sometimes prop one another up, and cheer one another on. And when we serve together, the love of God reaches out to others in ways that make us feel as though we're the ones being blessed even as we seek to bless others.

Meg serves with a ministry at her church that turns the weekend messages into a curriculum for small groups to use in deeper study. "Before I got involved with this ministry, I was pretty much a loner when it came to writing. But serving with other believers, hearing the passion and energy they contribute to the editing sessions, reminds me it's not about how great my writing is—it's about the end user. Is it clear? Will it promote life-changing discussion? Working on a team is not only more fun, it assures us that the lessons will not be about any one person's ego. They are intended to grow the body of Christ."

What I'm recommending to you here is more than simply a fellowship—though that's important, too. We all need other believers in our lives. But serving together with others is the closest thing to true biblical community you will find. Consider the stories of Peter, who so often is mentioned in the same breath as John regarding their hugely successful preaching and healing ministry in the early church. And then there's the great apostle Paul, who always had a missionary partner (Paul and Barnabas; Paul and Silas) or even a team (Timothy, Titus, Luke, Demas, Mark, and others). Even when Paul was in prison, he met regularly with teams of believers for mutual encouragement, support, and fellowship (Acts 27:3; 28:14, 15, 30). Together these teams healed the sick, raised the dead, cast out demons, preached boldly, defied death, wrote what would become the New Testament, and turned the world upside down for Jesus. We might think of Jesus' apostles as super-Christians, but they were just ordinary people on an extraordinary mission for God. Today we are called to carry on their work—and we do that best when we serve in community, as they did.

The Clarifying Power of Community

At long last Frodo made it inside Mount Doom and stood trembling on the precipice of the mountain's volcanic flames. The moment had come at last. He held up the ring, dangling it over the edge—gazing at it, unable to let it go. Behind him stood Sam, crying, "Destroy it! . . . What are you waiting for? Just let it go!"

All along the dangerous journey from the Shire to that moment, as trials and temptations continually beat them back and threatened to derail their mission, Sam had reminded Frodo of what mattered most.

In the film, we watch the two hobbits wrestle with the ring and with Gollum, interspersed with scenes of their companions battling to the death with the enemy army. Neither Frodo nor Aragorn and the armies of the West could have accomplished their tasks alone. The army, greatly outnumbered and doomed to fail, battled to keep the enemy's attention and efforts away from Frodo and Sam and their vital task. And although Frodo and Sam couldn't hope to save themselves by completing their task, their triumph was the only thing that would save Aragorn and the army. Because they all selflessly served the good of others on the team, the entire team was successful. With the help of their teammates, each person was able to get his job done—a job that literally saved Middle Earth.

When Frodo, the critically important Ring-bearer, faltered at the end—his judgment and will clouded by the power and pull of the ring—it was clear-minded Sam who brought Frodo back to center, helping him to see what must be done and keeping him from giving in or giving up. What would Frodo have done had he been alone?

Likewise, when we serve in community, we gain friends and mentors who help us see our critical next steps. They become our spiritual life-support systems. Through their counsel, God speaks wisdom into our lives and brings new clarity to our unique life purposes. We may not be called to save Middle Earth, but we are called into spiritual battle every day with God's enemy. Don't think you can fight those battles alone.

I remember a time when I believed with all my heart that I was called to preach the gospel to huge crowds in stadiums—I had Billy Graham–size visions of grandeur. I envisioned myself on a platform in center field, my voice echoing through the stands. In my mind's eye, thousands of people would rise to their feet and slowly make the trip toward home plate to pledge their lives to Jesus. Maybe I was really just a frustrated ballplayer.

Then one day a friend—someone with whom I'd served and who had become a mentor to me—said, "Erik, that may be a plan God has for you one day, but it's not what he wants you to do now." I couldn't believe my ears. If I wanted to do this good thing, why wouldn't God also want me to be out there saving people by the truckload?

My wise friend challenged me: "Is there one moment you can point to in the last five years when God has opened a door to that dream?" My friend was absolutely right. He helped me realize that my dream was the result of my wanting to compensate for the emotional insecurities left by my abandonment by my dad all those years ago. Wow, it hurt. But I needed to hear it. Otherwise I might still be banging my head on walls and practicing my stadium voice with nobody listening. If I hadn't been serving in a community of fellow believers, all of them loving and longing to please God, I might never have made this priceless friendship.

Even the great apostle Peter lost perspective about what was truly important (the gospel message, not Jewish traditions) for a while and needed to be confronted and corrected by Paul (Galatians 2:11–14). It's not a black mark on our Christian service record to have a Christian brother or sister challenge our perspective or actions. It's a crucial system of checks and balances that God wisely built into the works to keep us from getting off track or falling on our faces. Proverbs 15:22 reminds us: "Plans fail for lack of counsel, but with many advisers they succeed." God gives us a team of advisers to keep us going forward on a straight line to victory. What a good thing!

Like Frodo's friends and mine, your community helps you to understand the you God made you to be—the one only you can be.

Making It Count

God means for us to "do life" together. Hear his words to us: "Let us think about each other and help each other to show love and do good deeds. You should not stay away from the church meetings, as some are doing, but you should meet together and encourage each other. Do this even more as you see the day coming" (Hebrews 10:24–25 NCV). We need to be listeners, and we need to hear the words others say to us in ways that help us readjust our lives and our priorities. God often speaks to us through others.

We need the support we find when we serve with others. In these groups we find prayer support, grow in our faith, and often have our needs met. If it were not for my team at church, many days I'd have a tough time getting through. We get advice from our group that's often both course- and life-altering—if we're honest with ourselves and willing to listen.

So here's what I want to conclude with today: If you're already being supported by a group, you know what I've been talking about. Stay with it! Receive and give back that life support. But if you're not, why not? What are you waiting for? Or is it that you're hiding? Whatever your reason or excuse, you're mostly hurting yourself. But beyond that, the rest of us are missing out on what you have to offer. So, please, find a way to get involved. Yes, there are risks. Yes, someone in the group might hurt your feelings now and then, or you might have disagreements. Who doesn't? I once heard it said that whenever you have two believers in a room, you have three opinions: mine, yours, and the Holy Spirit's. We all know who's right, so it's just a matter of opening our hearts to the truth.

We'll all have times when circumstances seem as desperate as they did for Frodo Baggins when he became the Ring-bearer—it's the nature of life. When we do, I hope and pray we can be as strong and courageous as Frodo, and as blessed to have someone like Sam on our team. The time to forge those friendships is while you're living everyday life in the Shire, before you're called to the edge of Mount Doom.

I urge you to do whatever it takes to develop that spiritual life-support system. When I first heard about this concept, I admit that I wasn't wild about it. Up until then, my life had been largely a series of bad relationships. I didn't understand why I needed a group. Today I thank God for the people who regularly sharpen my focus, refresh my spirit, and sometimes carry me to the top. We serve together and we love it.

Get yourself surrounded.

Let's pray . . . together.

Lord, thank you for our conversation today. Please help my friends to understand the need for a group to hold us up when we're weak or to cheer us on when we run toward a goal. People out there need what groups can provide them—whether it's Meals on Wheels, mobile church, or just a friendly face on the church campus. When we give through our groups, we receive so much more in return than we can ever hope or imagine. Let us know the blessing of serving in community, as you did, Lord Jesus, with your disciples. We ask this in your name. . . . Amen.

Having a regular group of people with whom you serve and grow is critical to your Christian life. But each of us also needs to invest what God has given us into the life of at least one other person. If we don't pass it on while we're here, one day the opportunity will be eternally lost. That's what we'll chat about over our coffee tomorrow. See you then!

DEPOSITS

Investing in Others

Let this be written for a future generation,
that a people not yet created may praise the LORD.
Psalm 102:18

Transformation in the world happens
when people are healed and start investing in other people.
—Michael W. Smith

YOUNG WALT DISNEY HAD a dream. At first it was no more than images in his mind, but they were there every morning when he woke up, and they danced continually in his mind. As he grew older, that dream began to take shape: *a place,* he thought, *where parents and children could have fun together.* The idea just wouldn't leave him alone. Already notorious for crazy ideas that his brother Roy somehow had to find money to bankroll, this time Walt had gone too far. Everyone thought he'd lost it. But Roy just couldn't say no to his kid brother, so they pursued his dream. They knocked on just about every financial door they could find, only to have those doors slammed in their faces.

Finally someone at the then-struggling ABC network said, "Come on in!" They worked out a deal, and eventually Walt's dream kingdom, Disneyland, became a reality—but not before he'd put just about every penny of his personal fortune into it, not to mention every waking hour. As we can see through the prism of history, that risk has paid off with dividends that extend far beyond Walt Disney's lifetime. But there's no denying that when it began, Walt was betting the farm.

Investments are like that. We put our money into some kind of dream, hoping for a big return on that investment down the road. But the fact of the matter is, we have no idea what that payday will bring. We may end up with a billion-dollar dream park or just learn a billion-dollar lesson. Even Walt had to fail a few times—and fall hard—before he found the key to making his kingdom a success.

As believers, the kingdom we're to invest in is heaven. Jesus said, "Don't store treasures for yourselves here on earth where moths and rust will destroy them and thieves can break in and steal them. But store your treasures in heaven where they cannot be destroyed by moths or rust and where thieves cannot break in and steal them. Your heart will be where your treasure is" (Matthew 6:19–21 NCV). That doesn't mean we can't enjoy nice things down here or even accumulate wealth in this world. But Jesus understood that it's our nature to put our resources into those things we love most. Heaven, he explained, is the only place where those treasures will last.

Relational Deposits

We can find many ways and places to invest our lives for God's kingdom and Christ's sake. If you're not sure where to start, consider your sphere of influence—your family, your friends, your coworkers. Invite them to church or to a Bible study. Consider a weekly lunchtime fellowship where you work or go to school.

You'll find other ways to live out that influence, too, besides the typical avenues of church or some other Bible-centered arena. For instance, I know some guys who love to go to ball games. When they buy tickets, they always get at least one extra to invite someone along from outside their group. It's amazing what can happen in a person's life when he gets to witness love in action, and nothing quite expresses the love of God to a man like watching a band of brothers doing what Christian brothers do best—holding one another up and just enjoying one another's company.

We discussed leadership earlier in the book. Well, nowhere is your role as a leader better defined than when you choose to invest in others. You don't have to be a boss or a person with an official title to be a leader. You simply must be someone who works deliberately to influence others. At work, people watch the attitude with which you accept assignments and the way you speak to coworkers. Are you doing your job to the best of your abilities, or are you goofing off? What kinds of marks do you receive on your performance reviews? How did you react when the boss said the company would be cutting back and your job wasn't needed anymore? Moments such as these are opportunities for you to be a leader in the workplace simply by showing others how a Christ follower lives. This may sound like a cliché, but it's true nonetheless: people who would never pick up a Bible will read the gospel according to you.

Okay, now for a little exercise. Think about people whose lives you already influence, whom you can invest in. Who are these people? Where are they? In what specific ways can you make deposits in their lives for eternity? In the figure of concentric circles in the space below, write your name in the center.

Relational Circles

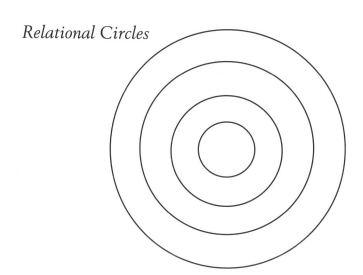

With whom are you likely to have the most influence? For me, it's my wife and kids. Write those names in the next circle from the center.

Now think of people in whose lives you've earned the right to speak truth—people who respect you and who come to you for answers. Write their names in the third circle from the center.

Finally, consider those people in whose lives you have the least influence—the barista at the coffee shop, for example; your neighbors; the people you rub shoulders with only superficially or occasionally. List them in the outer circle.

How will you invest in each life in your circle? Think of some practical things you can do—starting today—to encourage, guide, and assist these people in positive ways. Make this your game plan.

This exercise is meant to help you see that there are all kinds of possibilities for you to "pay forward" the blessings you've received and invest in eternity by pouring yourself into others. Even those you impact least are still watching you. Consider how to best represent Christ everywhere you go, through all the pieces of your life puzzle. Like tossing a rock in a pond, the smallest deposits can ripple across an ocean of time.

Beyond Today

For nearly three weeks now, we've been learning about the gifts and ingredients God has placed inside each of us. Those pieces make up our personal, God-given treasures. So here's the question we'll let percolate today: how long do you want your fortune to last?

Following are the stories of four people who pondered that question—and decided to invest for eternity.

Christine: Breaking the Grip of Generational Poverty

It was time. Christine had spent twenty years building a successful career in the mortgage industry, and now it was time to give back to the world.

She would pay it forward by helping America's less privileged. Christine sold her business and marched toward her dream, confident in the plan God had laid on her heart.

All her life, she'd traveled at high speed, making things happen and getting deals done. Why would it be any different now that she was ready to give full-time attention to God's purpose in her life? But after six months of knocking on doors to see which one would open, her knuckles were raw and not one door had budged. What was God doing here? Why wasn't this deal closing? Had she been wrong to give up her mortgage business to go after a dream she couldn't even name? Had she made a poor decision? Didn't God want to use her to make an impact for him? Maybe she should just give up, she thought.

Or maybe she should just slow down. That was the advice I gave her when she brought her questions to me. "God can't speak to you if you're constantly red-lining," I told her. "You can hear him best if you idle your engines awhile."

As we talked she began to see that there was an open door in front of her. It was an opportunity to take a new venture to the next level. Her husband had said, "Go for it!" and God had used me to confirm it. Today she is using her leadership gifts, business connections, and passion for the less fortunate by serving with Lift Up America, an organization that unites corporate America and grassroots organizations with the working poor and families mired in poverty for generations. The goal is to break kids out of the poverty cycle by giving them hope. Christine is investing in a better future for kids—and their kids after them—not by giving them a handout but by giving them a hand up.

Leon: Building Tomorrow's Builders

Leon loved watching young eyes light up as they discovered life's amazing truths and learned to apply information and knowledge. That love eventually became his life's work. Today, he reflects, "As a college professor I look for every opportunity to invest in my students. They are the next generation of leaders and need to learn beyond the books. I strive to teach my students life skills so they can make smart choices after they graduate. So I focus on building into them critical skills like decision making, team building, communication, conflict resolution, and goal setting, just to name a few. I endeavor to give them the tools to succeed in all areas of life."

Leon has grasped his place in time as a part of God's unfolding story. Unless we pass on what we know, the bridges that future generations need may not hold them up for long. Leon's treasure—his personal uniqueness—is being invested in what will last.

Connie: Mentoring Tomorrow's Mentors

As Connie was reaching the empty-nest stage in life, she decided to pursue an idea. "I love mentoring young women," she told me. "I'm not talking about a formal mentoring program, but lifestyle mentoring. Here's how I do it: I ask these young women to join me while I shop, do errands, and go to church. I want them to see the love of Jesus through me as I go about my life. In no way am I perfect, and I want them to realize that they don't need to be perfect, either—just be the person God made them to be. We laugh together, pray together, and simply do life together."

Connie doesn't go out in the streets to find these young women. They are her daughters and nieces, their friends, or young women from her church. She has become so well known for her warm, witty, and friendly ways that young women seek her out to be their mentor.

"This passion for developing young women led me to start my own program to help other women my age find a simple way to start investing in younger lives," she explained. "I call the program Walk with Me. God has used it to bless many people's lives. It's great to see more and more women my age finding fulfillment this way—by investing in the lives of few young women in their sphere of influence."

By using what God gave her, Connie is storing up lasting treasure in the best way possible—a way that multiplies its effectiveness. As the older women learn to become mentors, more young women benefit. And as these young women are mentored, they become qualified to mentor others. The blessing is paid forward to perhaps countless generations. What an investment!

Jason: Talking Teens through Life

Every now and then I meet adults who actually enjoy being around teenagers. Jason is one of them. "I love investing in these kids," he said. "They are so real and so raw with their feelings. They're not looking for people to be perfect—they don't even like the idea of perfect. They just need someone to help them talk through life situations."

Jason's interest in young people motivates his life choices, leading him to prioritize his time in ways that are likely to pay off richly down the road. "I look for ways to invest in them at church and in my community. Working as a volunteer leader for junior-high students during the weekend gives me a great platform to speak into their lives. I also lead a neighborhood Bible study with a group of teenagers. I look forward to our weekly meetings to study, to 'hang,' and to just be real together."

Investing in Tomorrow

Christine, Leon, Connie, and Jason are taking risks by choosing to invest their lives in the next generation. They have no guarantee that the time, energy, and love they pour out will come back to them in any way. Young people have a way of breaking our hearts, so it's possible that a few of Leon's students will flunk out or that some of Connie's girls will walk away from the example she so diligently sets. Christine's nonprofit idea could have failed. A percentage of the kids into whom Jason pours his life may not make the good choices he hopes they will. Those are the chances we take when we choose to engage in life at any level. But by surrendering their lives to the Lord and choosing to steward their uniqueness to its maximum effectiveness, our models are serving on

Christ's mission field, investing in the future, paying their lives forward, and storing up great treasure in heaven.

Because of people like Christine, Leon, Connie, and Jason, others benefit greatly. As a young man named James testifies, "I have been so blessed by having mentors in my life. I truly don't know where I would be today if I didn't have people I can call on at any time of the day for support. Sometimes they just talk me through a decision I'm facing or teach me how to treat my wife the way God intended. My pastor says we are 'better together,' and I am living proof. I'm a better man, better husband, and better leader because of the people who've unselfishly invested in my life."

Let me ask you again: how long do you want your treasure to last? Invest your life—and your riches—accordingly.

Making It Count

One of my favorite ways to pay it forward or invest in others is through books. Reading, as one friend of mine has said, is a way to connect people across generations. We can read about people who lived before our time and about ideas to make the world better going forward. Books touch our lives as few other tools can. Where else do people pour out their hearts and minds so personally and powerfully? I especially love handing out copies of books that have impacted my life.

What are your favorite books, and what people do you know who would love to read them, too? Maybe by now you realize someone in your life that needs their own copy of *Only You Can Be You*. If so, buy a copy and pass it on.

Another great way to store up eternal treasure is through the simple act of encouraging others. Paul spoke of his behavior and that of his company before the church at Thessalonica with these words: "You are witnesses, and so is God, of how holy, righteous and blameless we were among you who believed. For you know that we dealt with each of you as a father deals with his own children, encouraging, comforting and urging you to live lives worthy of God, who calls you into his kingdom and glory" (1 Thessalonians 2:10–12). Everyone needs to hear a word of good cheer now and then. Next time you walk into church, I want you to consider this likely possibility: out of every ten people you see, at least eight are going through a rough time right now. Even if you've never seen them before, you can speak a few words or give them a smile that will brighten their day. At home I think of encouraging my kids as giving them verbal vitamins every day. It fortifies their lives for whatever the cruel world might throw in their pathway. Whom can you fortify today in a way only you can do?

One of the best ways to invest in others' lives is through prayer. Over and over in the scriptures, we see Jesus modeling prayer for his disciples. In John 17 he prayed for himself, his disciples, and believers everywhere. Those words are among the most comforting in all the Bible.

In his model prayer, Jesus taught us to pray to the Father: "Your kingdom come, your will be done on earth as it is in heaven" (Matthew 6:10). So when we pray for and with others, we are literally inviting heaven into their lives. There is no better example of paying it forward than that.

What I want to leave you with today is simply a challenge to look for ways to invest your treasure in heaven instead of burying it here on earth. Now that you've discovered, surrendered, and begun stewarding your treasure for God, how can you best invest it for him? We posed that question last week, and by now I hope the answer is clear: you invest it best by sharing it with others. If God shows you someone to help, help that person. Look for open doors of opportunity. Ask people how you can help them. Look back at that Michael W. Smith quote we began with today. Where has God healed you? Apply that healing to someone else who's hurting. Be willing to go first, to take risks, and then surrender the outcome to God.

Let's pray.

Father, we come to you with full hearts, and we pour them out to you. Show us how we can best use those elements you have poured into our lives to build up treasure in heaven. How can we invest in your kingdom by using what you've given us here on earth? Help us to build bridges to heaven everywhere we go. As Jesus gave his life for others, show us how to give our lives, too. We ask this in Jesus' name. . . . Amen!

Okay, there's one last big idea I'd like to talk over with you before our time is up. Once we have a good idea of what God has put us here to do and we've got all our pieces in place, it's critical that we pull it all into some kind of order. After all, if our barista just poured every kind of coffee bean into the pot, we'd have a strange-tasting drink. Each roast might be good coffee, but blended together, the distinctive flavor of each bean would be lost. God wants the full flavor of our uniqueness to come out, and for that to happen, we have to understand how to prioritize our choices. Think that over, and we'll meet back here tomorrow.

Day 21

HOURGLASS

Prioritizing Your Life

Be diligent in these matters; give yourself wholly to them,
so that everyone may see your progress.
1 Timothy 4:15

Put first things first and we get second things thrown in:
put second things first and we lose both first and second things.
—C. S. Lewis

WHERE HAS THE TIME gone? Our three weeks together are almost up. In a way, though, this is just the beginning. Every day that God gives us breath is a new beginning, a new opportunity to choose whether we'll live for him or for ourselves. Each morning brings a brand-new occasion to surrender and to obtain a fresh dose of God's mercy and grace. Each day we get another 24 hours—168 hours each week. Because God has given us free will, what we do with those hours is our choice.

As the aroma of this coffee awakens your senses, let me ask you this: now that you have new perspective on your life, now that you know God made you to be exactly who you are and not like someone else, what will you do next? You can waste the time you've been given, or you can use it in the significant ways we've talked about. I hope you've surrendered the clutter and confusion in your life, the old sound tracks, the cravings, old ideas about your identity, and the relationships in your life—both the good and the bad. You've discovered that God intentionally created you with a unique set of talents, spiritual gifts, passions, experiences, and a winning personality; and you've got a good idea of the purpose for which he made you. You're on your way to realizing that you're not here for yourself but for the sake of others. So if you're committed to putting first things first, as author C. S. Lewis advised, how do you determine what those first things are? How can you know that you've ordered your life wisely?

The best way is to hold on to what you've learned in the past few weeks. Establish good spiritual habits. Just as daily exercise, a good diet, and regularly brushing your teeth are good physical habits, starting each day with God helps keep you healthy spiritually too. Develop a regular quiet time and place where you'll meet with God each day for instruction. David, who commanded Saul's armies and later became king of Israel, sought God's advice daily (Psalm 5:1–3). Why not think of yourself as a general in God's army, the way David did?

Beyond your basic decisions, ask yourself these key questions:

- What do I need to stop doing?
- What tasks do I need to shift to someone else?
- What do I need to start doing?

Once you've determined these answers for yourself, I suggest you revisit the questions periodically—perhaps at the beginning of each season—to reevaluate your direction and make sure you're keeping in step with God. Put the dates for these reviews on your calendar to make sure you don't forget them.

Always give yourselves fully
to the work of the Lord, because you know
that your labor in the Lord is not in vain.
1 Corinthians 15:58

Taking It In

Perhaps what I'm suggesting sounds to you like it'll increase your workload. "Add more to my day?" you might say. "How can I possibly find room for more?" Sure, you're busy, but if you're too busy for what's most important, you're in trouble. You'll just get busier and busier and less and less productive if you don't take a little time to "sharpen the ax."

Following are some tips to help you prioritize some of the really important things in life and keep your spiritual ax sharp and effective for the work to which God has called you.

Keeping A Daily Time with God

"If Satan can't make you bad," Cheryl's pastor told her, "he'll make you busy." Grasping that truth helped this on-the-go corporate executive start to better prioritize her life. "God calls me to give him the first part of my day, which I do as I drive to work each morning. I use that thirty-minute drive to pray and connect with my Lord."

If you've just got to rush out the door every morning on your way to work, think about how to double up your preparation time, as Cheryl did. Listen to devotionals on your iPod while you dress or to the Bible on CD. However you choose to do it, make sure you take time to surrender your day to God every day. I promise you'll notice the difference when you do—and when you don't.

Stay Connected

To grow and stay healthy, be sure to prioritize church attendance and small-group participation somewhere in your week. Plugging in to a small group is a way to make church more personal and to become connected to those people we talked about on Day 19—the ones with whom you'll "do life" together.

Minister

The rest of the week, go out and "do" church—engage with your culture, serve others, perform ministry, and accomplish your purpose in life.

Take Time Away

Solitude with God is crucial to our growth, and it sets the stage for how God can use us to reach the world. Without a functioning navigation system, boats and airplanes tend to drift off course. It's the same with us, so we've got to plan time in our lives to regularly check our compass settings. Robyn, for example, takes regular personal retreats—times away with just God and her Bible. Tom has a favorite quiet place he goes to whenever he can to simply wait on God and receive direction.

What I'm talking about is an attitude of expectation that prepares our hearts to hear God when he does speak. If we set aside that time to wait, then—whether we hear from God in that time frame or not—our spiritual "ears" are tuned in to hear him. The point is to be ready when God calls us. That takes preparation.

For three years, my wife, Stacey, and I were uninvolved church members. I sat and I soaked. We tried to find other young couples to connect with but weren't having much success. Then I learned of a need for a young married fellowship coordinator, and I volunteered. Before long the fellowship grew from three small groups to more than forty. When I was offered a staff position, Stacey and I prayed about it for ninety days. We wanted to honor God, but we also wanted to honor one of our most critical family values—that Stacey stay home to raise the kids. Debt from a student loan presented a major obstacle to living on the salary the church offered us. So we prayed for God to reveal his will. Ultimately I got a bonus that wiped out both our debt and our excuse. I spent the next three years completing my seminary degree as a member of the church staff. Do you think God was doing something? I have no doubt. It's how he directs our steps. God builds us up as we open up, so he can lift us up to that special place he created just for us. It's an old saying because it's true: where God guides, God provides.

Letting It Out

As you feast on God's mercy and grace for your life, remember that God has put you in the world to do his work. Before Jesus ascended into heaven, he made it clear to his disciples that they were to continue where he left off. Just ten days later, at Pentecost, the church was created (Acts 2), and while it has morphed and split and changed countless times over the past two thousand years, our mission has remained the same: "Go and make disciples of all nations, baptizing them in the name of the Father and of the Son and of the Holy Spirit, and teaching them to obey everything I have commanded you" (Matthew 28:19–20).

We are called to go. No matter what God has wired into the special package called you, your ultimate mission is to go—not to stay in one place or to keep his good news to yourself. So, as God feeds you, be sure to find a way to pour it back into the lives of others. In a world that's looking for God in all the wrong places, realize that God intends you to reveal him to those around you by modeling Christ through your life.

God has made many ways for you to express the uniqueness that is you, and all of them involve your highest purpose—to give your life away for Jesus' sake. Sharing the good news of Christ is our overarching reason for living. Here's another of those old mottoes: good works create goodwill and open the door for the good news.

So how do we begin to share this good news? The gospel of Mark records a story of a man Jesus healed of leprosy, a disfiguring and potentially deforming disease primarily of the skin. Because leprosy was believed to be highly contagious, those afflicted with the disease were separated from society—cast out, cast off, with no human contact, left to die alone. Wherever these lepers went, they were required to cover their faces and warn others to avoid them by crying out, "Unclean! Unclean!"

One day a leper, having heard of Jesus, sought him out and begged him for help: "If you are willing, you can make me clean" (Mark 1:40). Jesus was filled with compassion for the man and healed him, warning him as he did: "See that you don't tell this to anyone" (Mark 1:44).

But such a wondrous thing had happened to him that the leper couldn't hold the good news inside! He had to share this amazing news with others. That's the way it should be with us. Spiritually, we were all unclean "lepers" until Christ touched us and made us clean. That dramatic change is bound to show in our lives, especially with those who have known us best. Be ready to tell them who has healed you and given you new life. Like the dramatically healed leper in the Bible, we shouldn't be able to keep quiet about such a great thing that God has done for us.

Sharing with others the good news of God's love and restorative power must be a priority in our lives. We must live every day in such a way that those we encounter have no doubt about the impact Jesus has had on our lives—and can have on theirs. Which people should be our first priority for sharing this message?

Our Families

Here's how Cheryl, our busy executive, makes sure her family sees Christ in her life: "I make sure to call my two grown daughters two or three times a week so I can pray for them. I also make sure to check in with my husband every day so I can let him know how much I love him. Finally, I make sure to check in with my three grandkids. The greatest reward to prioritizing my relationships has been love, joy, and the fulfillment it brings to my life." You can believe Cheryl's family is well aware of who has changed her life so wonderfully. Does your family know as clearly?

The World

Beyond our families, God has called us to go into the world. "You will receive power when the Holy Spirit comes on you; and you will be my witnesses in Jerusalem, and in all Judea and Samaria, and to the ends of the earth," Jesus told his followers in Acts 1:8, just before he was taken up into heaven. What that requires of you involves all the things we've been talking about for the past three weeks: your surrendered, well-stewarded life and your decision to use what God has given you in Christ's service. You accomplish that mission by diligently listening for his direction and stepping out in faith.

How do you determine what matters most in life? You acknowledge that God has made you for a special purpose, you surrender your life to him for that purpose, you use what he's given you responsibly to serve others—and you listen, just as Cheryl has trained herself to do, just as Jesus stole away in the quiet hours of the morning to do (Mark 1:35).

Making It Count

If a message resonates with your heart in a big way, you owe it to God to explore the reasons. Consider how one young man is already maximizing his lifetime joy potential:

Zach unashamedly introduces himself as an abolitionist. At first blush we're tempted to say, "But slavery was abolished almost 150 years ago!" Zach wants you to know that it wasn't. In the United States and much of the Western world it was, perhaps, but the cruel practice is still carried out in much of the rest of the world. When he learned about all the people (mostly women and children) still being forced into slavery,

Zach knew he had to do something about it. So he started a foundation called Loose Change to Loosen Chains (LC2LC). On the LC2LC MySpace page, Zach says of his mission:

> I felt a need to do something to bring freedom to the victims I was learning about. LC2LC is a group of students and emerging leaders who want to see the trade in human beings stopped. Modern-day slavery may be people working in brick kilns, rice mills, fishing villages or brothels.
>
> Together we can make a difference. Let's abolish slavery!"[1]

Zach began this mission when he was in the seventh grade and runs it now with his parents' support. Zach Hunter is just fifteen years old, yet he is already making a difference with his life. Where priorities are concerned, you could say he is way ahead on God's learning curve. Having already attained a life of significance, Zach is ready for Day 22. Are you?

As we conclude our twenty-one days together, would you pray with me?

Lord, thank you for walking with me on this journey these past few weeks and for opening my eyes to the wonderful way you have made me. Thank you for the stories of my fellow travelers on this earth—people who have hungered after you, who have sought you and longed to please you with their lives. Father, give me that kind of heart—a heart to please you by serving others in this world, by reaching out with your truth and your good news to share with those still in darkness. Let me be one who turns on your light for others. And then open their eyes to see that this light is named Jesus. Amen.

AFTERWORD

Living with Purpose

EYE ON THE PRIZE

Sustaining Significance

It's crucial that we keep a firm grip
on what we've heard so that we don't drift off.
Hebrews 2:1 MSG

Let your religion be less of a theory and more of a love affair.
—G.K. Chesterton

IN THE MOVIE *The Greatest Game Ever Played,* the relationship between young amateur golfer Francis Ouimet and his even younger caddy, the fifth-grader named Eddie, captivated me. During that historic 1913 U.S. Open tournament portrayed in the film, whenever Ouimet was starting to get distracted by comparing his performance with those of others, Eddie would bring his attention back around to what mattered most. "Read it, roll it, hole it," he wisely said. Ouimet had a good, strong record going into that match, but he needed to stay focused in order to sustain what he had achieved. Eddie's advice kept him zeroed in on what mattered most.

Too many people fail to reach their goals because they get distracted and then discouraged. Making it all the way to the finish line is hard work! But we've got to keep our eyes on the prize. When we find ourselves within reach of our goal, we have to stay focused in order to make it all the way to that finish line . . . or to the eighteenth hole. In other words, like Ouimet, we must learn to read it, roll it, and hole it.

Now that you've surrendered your life and taken hold of your spiritual gifts, abilities, passions, experiences, and personality, you can no longer say, "I don't know who I am." Unless the caffeine hasn't kicked in and you've been sleeping these past three weeks, you now have a good idea why God put you here, and you realize that you have a responsibility to give back to God. Our three weeks together may be over, but you're really just at the beginning of doing what you were meant to do. Now you know you can't be just anything you want to be, but you can be exactly who God made you to be.

If you're serious about being the you God made you to be, you have to remain engaged and determined to make a difference. It's one thing to discover your purpose in life; it's quite another to continue seeking to become all you are meant to be—what the apostle Paul called pressing toward the goal (Philippians 3:14). It won't always be easy, so if we are to sustain the significance for which God created us, we must persevere. Walt Disney called it "stick-to-itivity." That's a great word. If you stick to it, you'll be able to complete the task before you. If you keep your head down and your eye on the ball, you'll sink that putt eventually.

When it comes to sustaining significance, we must take on the attitude of Paul, who understood that we all are works of God in progress. He wrote, "I'm not saying that I have this all together, that I have it made. But I am well on my way, reaching out for Christ, who has so wondrously reached out for me. Friends, don't get me wrong: By no means do I count myself an expert in all of this, but I've got my eye on the goal, where God is beckoning us onward—to Jesus. I'm off and running, and I'm not turning back" (Philippians 3:12–14 MSG). When we reach out for Christ, we'll find that his arms are more than sufficient to hold us.

Donna reached out to Christ in a time of crisis and found him wondrously reaching out for her too. In the middle of her tragedy, God was faithful to bring Donna a new realization of her purpose and significance in him. It wasn't easy. At first Donna wasn't sure how she would make it through the day, much less whatever was left of her life. She and her husband, Pat, were in Ireland to bury his mother when Pat suffered a massive heart attack. He didn't recover. Donna and Pat had moved to a new community just months earlier. They hadn't had time to make friends, much less put down roots, and then Pat had been called home. "Why, God, why?" Donna cried out in desperation. But "why" is not something God is in the habit of disclosing. He is, however, in the business of changing lives and hearts, as Donna was about to learn.

"One day," she said, "the pastor of my church called me to his office about a job that was available. I was a new member! Why would he call me? Now, three years later, I've been able to work and learn at the same time. God put me here and has held me close. I still don't know the why, but I've learned, among many other things, that I don't have to know why. All the fruits of the Spirit are mine to claim. I wait with God-given patience and joy for what he has in store for me. I never knew that I could praise him even through the heartache, but I do now. God has shown me great things, and I can hardly wait to pass them on to others." Donna is learning to keep her eyes on the prize.

A life of sustained significance is not one without pain, but it is one in which we experience God's faithfulness amid the pain and receive his healing balm wherever we need it. And it's a life of indescribable joy—a joy like that of the leper in Mark 1—joy that cannot be contained. Most of all, your life of sustained significance is a life that no one else can live quite like you. You live this uniquely significant life by choosing to be the you God made you to be every day he gives you life.

Making It Count

I am the vine, and you are the branches.
If any remain in me and I remain in them,
they produce much fruit. But without me
they can do nothing.
John 15:5 NCV

Remember the goal you set back at the very beginning of our journey together, on page 21? Turn to that page now and see if you've been able to achieve your goal with God's help.

Now that our three weeks together are at an end, make sure you plan at least one next step toward that sustained life of significance for which God created you. Choose from my list, or think up something on your own to cement your decision.

- *Celebrate your achievement with God.* Write him a letter. Develop a praise report of all the wonderful things God did in you and through you over the last twenty-one days.
- *Connect with your circle of support,* those special folks you identified back on Day 19 and with whom you'll be doing life together. If you already have a group, great. Communicate to them what you've learned. If not, please do what it takes to find one.
- *Challenge a friend to walk through this book with you* and find freedom and fulfillment in his or her life, too. When you share what you've learned with someone else, you pay it forward to at least one more life.
- *Cultivate your relationship with God.* Secure your connection and ensure that your life truly counts by spending time with

God daily in Bible study and prayer. Helen, one of the most vibrant believers I know, told me she gets up every morning at five and spends the next hour and a half with God, either listening to praise music on her iPod, praying, reading God's Word, or a combination of the three. The thought of getting up that early may make you groan, but Helen wants you to know that it is possible, and the payoff is well worth the effort. The point is to do something—schedule that regular time with God in your day whenever and however you can. It doesn't need to be an hour and a half—it can be five minutes or thirty, whatever works for you. What matters is that you do it. Give God the best part of your day, every day, and watch him multiply the return on that investment.

Be sure to check your progress regularly. Each month set aside a few minutes to evaluate your life to ensure that your *one* life is focused on *two* goals ("Love the Lord your God with all your heart and with all your soul and with all your strength and with all your mind" and "Love your neighbor as yourself") and hallmarked by *three* choices: surrender, stewardship, and service.

Finally, determine to live each day completely in love with God. If you give him first place in your life, you'll be living with right priorities. Everything else will fall in line behind it.

Christ is the visible image of the invisible God. He existed before anything was created and is supreme over all creation, for through him God created everything in the heavenly realms and on earth. He made the things we can see and the things we can't see—such as thrones, kingdoms, rulers, and authorities in the unseen world. Everything was created

through him and for him. He existed before
anything else, and he holds
all creation together.
Colossians 1:15–17 NLT

Years ago I learned in a college exercise-physiology class about a substance in our bodies called laminin. I'd forgotten the name until I saw a YouTube video recently that reminded me. In it, Pastor Louie Giglio, describing to his listeners a God who breathes out the stars and literally holds our lives together, tells of meeting a molecular biologist who told him about laminin. When he got home and Googled it, Giglio was stunned by the image that confronted him—for the laminin model was shaped unmistakably like a cross. It became the visual proof for Giglio's message. Wikipedia says that laminins are "a family of glycoproteins that are an integral part of the structural scaffolding in basement membranes in almost every animal tissue." It further explains that laminin "is vital to making sure overall body structures hold together."[1] Laminin literally holds your body together, much the way God, through Christ, takes all the ingredients that make up you, fits them all perfectly into place, and holds them together so that you might become all he wants you to be. That's how much God loves you!

Let's keep focused on that goal, those of us
who want everything God has for us. If any of
you have something else in mind, something
less than total commitment, God will clear
your blurred vision—you'll see it yet! Now
that we're on the right track, let's stay on it.
Philippians 3:15–16 MSG

Would you pray with me one last time?

God, what an amazing adventure these past three weeks have been! Thank you for showing me that you have made me to be a distinctly unique individual and that you've intended all along that I should live my one and only life for you. It seems all the other messages I hear are telling me the opposite—that I'm expendable, replaceable, just a number or a square on an organizational chart. But you say that I'm special, unique, and not an accident of nature. Thank you for piercing through the noise and penetrating my heart. Help me now to live every day of this life for you by reaching out to this lost world with your message of hope. You've shown me that you long for me to be Christ's ambassador to the others in my life. Help me to be faithful in that mission. I ask it in Jesus' beautiful and precious name. Amen.

At the beginning of our time together I told you about the brief life of little Lea, gone after only four months on earth. Yet her life made a difference. The truth is, we are all here for only a moment. God wants you to use your time well. He longs for you to reach the pinnacle for which he uniquely created you.

Will you do it? Are you in? After all, only you can be you.

APPENDIX

What's in Your Box?

Assessing Your God-given Tools

FINDING YOUR ROLE

G OD HAS GIFTED US with a number of abilities. Look over this list of roles and determine which ones fit you. Then create a top-ten list and start using these strengths to make a difference for God.

- **Adapter:** You can easily adjust to new situations. Changes, alterations, and modifications don't make you break a sweat.
- **Administrator:** When someone is needed to run the show, you're the one most frequently called upon. You're good at governing or ruling the program.
- **Analyst:** You're a regular Sherlock Holmes, gifted at investigating, probing, examining, and evaluating situations.
- **Builder:** You're good at making things with your hands, including construction and assembly.
- **Coach:** You have the ability to prepare, instruct, train, and equip others. You're good at helping them develop who they are meant to be.
- **Communicator:** You're good at getting the message out. You love to share or impart information.
- **Competitor:** You love to enter contests of any kind, and you'll do what it takes to get to the finish line first. Most of all, you like to win.
- **Computer:** Who needs a calculator? You have a natural ability with numbers and love to add or estimate.
- **Connector:** You're a natural at pairing people up or getting them networked in groups. Relationships matter to you.
- **Consultant:** You're the one people come to for advice or to discuss matters, either personal or professional.
- **Cook:** Friends say you should have your own show on the cooking

channel or your own catering business. You love preparing and serving food.

- **Coordinator:** You know what goes together when it comes to mixing, matching, and harmonizing.
- **Counselor:** You are frequently sought out for advice, moral support, or a shoulder to cry on. People know you will listen to them and that you truly care.
- **Decorator:** Martha Stewart, move over! You love to enhance and beautify your surroundings.
- **Designer:** You like to draw, create, or organize graphics. Get the picture?
- **Developer:** When you get involved, projects grow, increase, or expand.
- **Director:** You're a natural when it comes to managing or supervising a project. You understand how to oversee resources to achieve a goal or an aim.
- **Editor:** You're gifted at knowing what needs to be corrected, altered, or amended to improve a creative project.
- **Encourager:** You have a reputation as one who supports others, cheering them on and inspiring them.
- **Engineer:** You're gifted when it comes to designing, planning, and construction.
- **Facilitator:** In a group setting, you're the one who gets the ball rolling. You have an ability to aid, assist, or get things going.
- **Forecaster:** You have a natural ability to see trends and patterns and predict what will happen.
- **Implementer:** You're the one people call when a plan needs to be executed. You know how to make things happen.
- **Improver:** You see how to make a situation better by enhancing or enriching it.
- **Influencer:** You're naturally able to sway opinion or to mold, shape, or change a situation or an atmosphere.
- **Landscaper:** You're at home in the garden and love to improve property.

- **Leader:** You know how to pave the way for others and direct them along a winning path.
- **Learner:** Information is your hobby. You love to study, gather information, and understand how things work.
- **Manager:** You're good at overseeing teams or projects.
- **Mentor:** You enjoy guiding the growth of others by teaching and/or advising them.
- **Motivator:** Your words and/or actions help stir others into action.
- **Negotiator:** You're good at settling arguments or mediating discussions.
- **Operator:** Running mechanical or technical instruments comes easily to you.
- **Organizer:** You have an ability to simplify life for yourself and others by arranging, fixing, classifying, or coordinating.
- **Performer:** You are gifted at singing, speaking, dancing, playing instruments, and any of the theatrical arts.
- **Pioneer:** You thrive on new endeavors—the more ground-breaking and original, the better.
- **Planner:** You like to map out your adventures and are good at making preparations.
- **Promoter:** You're a natural-born salesperson, gifted at showcasing, sponsoring, and endorsing people, projects, and products.
- **Recruiter:** You are good at enlisting people for a role, project, or team. Recruiters know how to hire, draft, and engage the skills of others.
- **Repairer:** Whether it's people or things, you know how to put things back together; to fix what's broken; to refurbish, restore, or heal.
- **Researcher:** You enjoy gathering information, studying topics, or examining facts.
- **Resourcer:** People count on you to deliver the goods. You provide the resources needed to get things accomplished.

- **Server:** Helping others fulfills you, too.
- **Strategist:** The wheels are always turning in your head, figuring out the next best move. You enjoy calculating and looking down the road.
- **Teacher:** When you speak, people listen and learn. You have an ability to explain or demonstrate how to do things. Tutoring others comes naturally.
- **Translator:** You know how to decipher other languages and help build bridges to understanding. You can interpret, decode, or explain what someone or something else means.
- **Traveler:** You are drawn to exploration and visiting other places and lands. The world fascinates you.
- **Visualizer:** You see things before they become reality through your naturally creative ability to imagine the future. You relate to life visually and enjoy dreaming of what could be.
- **Welcomer:** People feel warmed by your presence as you greet them and welcome them, either into your home, church, or place of business. People are comfortable around you.
- **Writer:** Words fascinate you. You love stringing them together any way you can. You're good at composing stories, communicating messages, and keeping records.

My top 10 talents:

1. _____   6. _____
2. _____   7. _____
3. _____   8. _____
4. _____   9. _____
5. _____   10. _____

EXPLANATION
OF SPIRITUAL GIFTS

Administration—This God-given ability serves and strengthens the body of Christ by effectively organizing both people and resources in order to reach ministry goals. If this is your gift, you might be:

- An effective organizer
- Known for being an efficient planner who reaches your goals
- A natural delegator
- Someone who looks for opportunities to make decisions
- A person who sees what needs to be done in order for dreams to become reality

Apostleship—A person with this gift is good at launching and leading new ministry endeavors for the purpose of advancing God's kingdom. The original Greek word for *apostle* means "sent one." If this is your gift, you might be:

- Driven to start new endeavors, most often churches, for God
- Open to risky new challenges
- Someone who enjoys making a difference in the lives of both believers and nonbelievers
- Eager to be known as one of Christ's ambassadors to the world
- A person who enjoys working hard to help churches reach their full potential for God

Discernment—God gives us this ability to help us recognize truth or error within a message, a person, or an event. If this is your gift, you might be:

- Someone who easily "reads" people and who is usually right
- Able to recognize whether a message is from God, Satan, or man
- Able to recognize inconsistencies in others
- Someone who easily identifies another's true motives or agenda
- Able to perceive when the truth is communicated with error or is being twisted

Encouragement—Some people are naturally able to inspire and encourage others. They often serve as counselors or people who empower others to achieve their God-given dreams. If this is your gift, you might be:

- One who inspires others to live for Christ
- Easily able to rejoice with those who have overcome difficult life situations through Christ's help
- Someone who seeks out opportunities to help others reach their full potential in Christ
- A natural encourager, whether through your words or your actions
- One who readily rejoices at others' success

Evangelism—People who share the love of Christ with others in a way that draws them to accept Christ's gift of eternal life display the gift of evangelism. If this is your gift, you might be:

- A person who looks for ways to build relational bridges with nonbelievers

- Able to sense when a person might be open to hear and receive the gospel
- Someone who's seen many people come to faith in Christ
- Able to triumph over logical arguments, winning others to Christ simply by loving them
- Someone who is deeply concerned for people who don't yet know Jesus

Faith—People with this gift are able to trust God to handle any and all obstacles along the way to accomplishing his purposes. If this is your gift, you might be:

- A person who welcomes the opportunity to take risks for God
- Energized by volatile situations
- Challenged by ideas and situations that most people see as impossible
- Often seen by others as having a passionate prayer life
- Someone able to embark on ventures with great God-confidence

Giving—This gift is characterized by the ability to joyfully support and fund initiatives for building God's kingdom through support that goes above and beyond the regular tithe. If this is your gift, you might be:

- Able and willing to intentionally give more than the 10 percent tithe in order to advance efforts you see as growing God's kingdom
- Someone who prefers your donations to remain anonymous whenever possible
- A person who seeks out ways to increase your resources in order to give more for God's use

- Someone who sees your resources as tools given by God for his use

Healing—People with this gift are able to heal and restore physical health to others by means other than the traditional or natural. If this is your gift, you might be:

- A person who firmly believes that people can be supernaturally healed
- Someone who prays to be used by God for the purpose of healing others
- Able to realize without question that healing occurs only by God's divine permission
- Someone who views traditional medicine as one way God may choose for healing
- Able to embrace this gift as from the hand of God and to see it specifically as a way to bring him glory

Helping—People with this gift enjoy assisting others in reaching goals that glorify God and strengthen the body of Christ. It is sometimes called the gift of helps or service. If this is your gift, you might be:

- A person who enjoys and looks for ways to help out behind the scenes
- Someone who rejoices in the success of others
- Detail oriented
- Often in search of ways to assist others
- Not interested in recognition for what you do

Hospitality—A person with this gift enjoys providing others with a warm and welcoming environment for fellowship. If this is your gift, you might be:

- Known for making others feel valued and cared for
- Always on the lookout for people who may go unnoticed in a crowd
- Someone who wants others to feel loved and welcomed
- Able to see your home as God's property for the express purpose of making others feel welcome
- Someone who promotes fellowship among others

Interpretation—People with this gift are able to understand a message from God delivered by another using a special language (see Tongues, page 250) unknown to others in attendance. If this is your gift, you might be:

- Able to perceive a clear idea of what God is saying through another person, even though the language the speaker is using is unknown to you.
- Able to translate words and messages of God in a way that edifies, comforts, and exhorts believers
- Able to communicate so as to make understood the sounds, words, and utterances made by others that glorify God

Knowledge—This is a gift to communicate God's truth to others in a way that promotes justice, honesty, and understanding. If this is your gift, you might be:

- Someone who devotes much of your time to reading Scripture
- A person who loves to share biblical insight
- One who enjoys helping others understand God's Word

- One who finds time spent studying and researching Scripture beneficial
- Someone who delights in answering difficult questions about God's Word

Leadership—This is the gift to cast vision, stimulate spiritual growth, apply strategies, and achieve success where God's purposes are concerned. If this is your gift, you might be:

- Given to huge visions for God and able to inspire others to work toward accomplishing those goals
- Naturally drawn into leadership roles
- A motivator who encourages both people and teams to work together to achieve God's purposes
- Naturally able to grasp the big picture
- Able to delegate responsibility to others who are qualified in order to get things done for God

Mercy—This gift involves ministering to those who suffer physically, emotionally, spiritually, or relationally. Its actions are characterized by love, care, compassion, and kindness toward others. If this is your gift, you might be:

- Drawn to opportunities that allow you to meet the needs of others in practical ways
- Able to devote significant prayer time on behalf of the needs of others
- Someone who puts the needs of others ahead of your own
- A person who grieves at the grief of others
- One who is most fulfilled by visiting people in need, whether in hospitals, nursing homes, orphanages, prisons, on the mission field, or wherever else God leads

Miracles—A person with this gift recognizes God's supernatural power to act in the natural world. If you have this gift, you might be:

- Able to view prayer as a supernatural vehicle through which God acts in the lives of people on earth
- Someone who gives credit to God alone for supernatural works
- Able to grasp fully that miracles occur only by God's will
- Someone who sees yourself as an instrument for God's use
- Someone who prays and expects supernatural results in "impossible" situations

Pastoring—A person gifted in pastoring takes spiritual responsibility for equipping a group of believers to live Christ-centered lives. *Shepherding* is another word used for this particular gift. If this is your gift, you might be:

- Driven to help others reach their full potential in Christ
- Someone who enjoys serving others and who looks for opportunities to serve
- Good at developing personal, trust-based relationships with others, particularly a small number of people
- Someone with a propensity for meeting the needs of others, willingly giving your time to help them with spiritual issues
- Someone who believes that people take precedence over projects

Prophecy—People with this gift are known for offering messages from God that comfort, encourage, guide, warn, or reveal sin in a way that leads to repentance and spiritual growth. The original Greek meaning of the word *prophecy* is "to speak forth the truth." The gift includes both forth-telling (preaching), and foretelling (revelation). If you have this gift, you might be:

- Known for publicly communicating God's Word, using a variety of means
- Someone who loves to share your strong biblical convictions with others
- A person who views yourself as God's tool, ready to be used by the Holy Spirit in changing lives
- Someone who finds it easy to confront others' motives when they are not up to God's standards
- A person who frequently receives and shares messages directly from God for comforting, challenging, or confronting his people

Teacher—This gift enables you to teach sound doctrine in relevant ways, empowering people to gain a sound and mature spiritual education. If you have this gift, you might be:

- Given to hours in the study of Scripture in order to best apply its principles and truth
- Someone who enjoys making the Bible clear and understandable to others
- A person who seeks out opportunities to speak biblical insight into daily situations
- Good at helping others learn to study the Bible
- Able to recognize a variety of ways to effectively communicate the Word of God, including speaking

Tongues—This gift enables a person to communicate God's message in a special language unknown to the speaker. If you have this gift, you might be:

- One who believes God is prompting you to communicate his message, often through prayer, in a specific language unknown to you

- Someone who intercedes for others in prayer using unknown words, sounds, and utterances
- One who desires and seeks out opportunities to pray, using these unknown languages for God's glory
- Ready to share with others the words and/or messages of God given to you in unknown languages
- Able to comfort or exhort others using unknown languages inspired by God

Wisdom—This gift is characterized by the ability to make wise decisions and to counsel others with sound advice, all in accordance with God's will. If this is your gift, you might be:

- One who enjoys speaking biblical insights into life situations
- Sought after by others for advice/wisdom
- One who takes pleasure in counseling others
- Known for making correct decisions and judgments
- Able to recognize God as the primary source of wisdom and direction

SMALL GROUP DISCUSSION QUESTIONS

I hope you'll take time to invite a few friends to join you here at the coffee shop or in someone's home, to dig deeper into getting to know the you God made you to be. Here are some questions to help spur discussion.

Week One Discussion Questions:
Surrendering Your Life Completely

Discuss with the group your thought of this week's video message from Erik. If you have not viewed this week's message please watch week one online at www.onlyyoucanbeyou.com.

Other discussion questions based on this week's reading:

- What does it mean to you today to realize God has made you for a specific purpose? How will this knowledge change the way you live tomorrow?
- How have past lies impacted your present? Discuss ways to replace those old sound tracks with God's truth and agree to check up on one another's progress.
- Can you name a few cravings that might not be God's best for you? How will you let God turn them into a hunger for the things of God?
- How could letting go of past pain and forgiving those who've hurt you help you become more of who God made you to be? What might the new you look like?
- How could releasing your roles into God's hands help you become more you?
- What do you think would happen if you gave your deepest desires to God? Why are you afraid to take this step? What's the worst that could happen if you did?

253

- What have you been holding on to that's keeping you from fully experiencing the new life God has for you? Confessing it to a friend is a good first step in letting it go.

Week Two Discussion:
Stewarding Your Unique Style Wisely

Discuss with the group your thought of this week's video message from Erik. If you have not viewed this week's message, please watch week two online at www.onlyyoucanbeyou.com.

Other discussion questions based on this week's reading:

- How could using your God-given uniqueness for his pleasure help you become more you? Share some of your struggles and ideas.
- If your current lifestyle isn't giving you opportunities to grow your God-given abilities, where can you go to discover what you to do best? Take a step this week.
- Consider "test-driving" a ministry or two at your church to find out what God has uniquely given you. If you've done that, share your experience with your group.
- Tell your group where God is stirring you to make a difference with your life. What ideas can you offer one another for moving ahead in search of that passion?
- How could God use your high-point experiences on page 131 to help someone else? What about the not-so-high-point moments you noted on page 135?
- What did you discover about your own special mix of ingredients on pages 142–143? Why do you think we need all personality types in God's kingdom?
- From page 151, what do you think God has put in your puzzle box? Is the complete picture beginning to show up? Share what God is revealing to you with your group.

Week Three Discussion:
Serving Others Passionately

Discuss with the group your thought of this week's video message from Erik. If you have not viewed this week's message, please watch week three online at www.onlyyoucanbeyou.com.

Other discussion questions based on this week's reading:

- What is the difference between Jesus' style of leadership and that of so many leaders today? How can a leader be a servant? Have you ever thought of yourself as a leader? What difference does that awareness make for you?

- Why do you think people are afraid or reluctant to help others today? How can a choice to help make you look more like Jesus—and more like the real you?

- Do you remember a time when you did not know Christ? How can recalling your own hungry days help you reach out to those who are starving spiritually?

- Have you begun to find true significance through serving? If so, how can your experience encourage others to do the same?

- Why do you think so many of us shy away from groups? What can you do to plug yourself into ministry and encourage others to do so as well, in spite of past issues?

- Have you ever received a blessing that went on to bless others as well, or do you know a story like the ones in this chapter? Share it briefly as an encouragement to invest in others.

- What will you do next as a result of spending the last three weeks on this adventure? How has God revealed his plan for your life? Are you ready to "pay it forward"? What is next for you? Share your plans with your group—and don't neglect to pray for one another.

NOTES

Introduction: Your Moment

1. John Ortberg, *When the Game Is Over, It All Goes Back in the Box* (Grand Rapids, MI: Zondervan, 2007).

2. *Merriam-Webster's Collegiate Dictionary,* 11th ed., s.v. "stewardship."

3. David Hochman, "Denzel Washington: Devoted to Family and Faith," http://www.rd.com.edgekey.net/your-america-inspiring-people-and-stories/denzel-washington-interview-devoted/article49236-2.html.

4. Rick Warren, *The Purpose Driven Life* (Grand Rapids, MI: Zondervan, 2002), 241.

Day 1: Restoration

1. Kay Warren, *Dangerous Surrender* (Grand Rapids, MI: Zondervan, 2007) 23.

Day 2: Surround Sound

1. Joyce Meyer, quoted on Quote Monk.com, http://www.quotemonk.com/quotes/self_quotes.htm (accessed September 26, 2008).

Day 3: Cravings

1. Kathi Macias, "Homesick?" March 24, 2008, http://www.kathimacias.com.

2. You can visit the Celebrate Recovery website at http://www.celebraterecovery.com.

Day 4: Scrapes and Scars

1. Lance Armstrong with Sally Jenkins, *It's Not About the Bike* (New York: Berkley Publishing Group, 2000, 2001), 2.

Day 5: Today

1. Nancy Lovell, "The Stopped Action Dream," FaithInTheWorkplace.com, Christianity Today International, http://www.christianitytoday.com/workplace/articles/interviews/philvischer.html (accessed September 26, 2008).

2. "What Is TSC?" Tuberous Sclerosis Alliance, http://www.tsalliance.org/pages.aspx?content=2 (accessed September 9, 2008).

3. Vik Jolly, "Patriotism, gratitude lead mom to give back," *Orange County Register,* January 24, 2008.

Day 6: Dreams and Desires

1. Dan Wooding, "Life Without Limbs," ASSIST News Service, March 12, 2008, http://www.assistnews.net/STORIES/2008/s08030074.htm (accessed September 12, 2008).

Day 8: Life on Loan

1. Tom Holladay, *Drive Time* devotions, Ephesians week three, day two, Monday, March 31, 2008.

Day 9: Treasure Chest

1. Cecil Murphey, "Comparing," email newsletter, March 4, 2008. Used by permission from the author.

2. Jim Collins, *Good to Great: Why Some Companies Make the Leap—and Others Don't* (New York: HarperBusiness, 2001).

3. Michael Sanders, "The Law of Differences: Life or Death for Relationships," Ministry Insights International, http://www.leadingfromyour strengths.com/articles/lawofdifferences.php.

4. Scott Reeves, "Loving the Job You Hate," Forbes.com, December 1, 2005, http://www.forbes.com/careers/2005/11/30/career-work-employment-cx_sr_1201bizbasics.html (accessed September 29, 2008).

Day 11: Jesus Calling

1. Pat Williams, http://www.patwilliamsmotivate.com (accessed October 2, 2008).

Day 13: Seasonings

1. John Trent, Rodney Cox, and Eric Tooker, *Parenting from Your Strengths* (Nashville, TN: Broadman & Holman, 2006).

2. Tom Paterson, *Living the Life You Were Meant to Live* (Nashville, TN: Thomas Nelson, 1998, 2003), 194.

Day 14: Inside the Box

1. Rick Rusaw and Eric Swanson, *Living a Life on Loan: Finding Grace at the Intersections* (Cincinnati, OH: Standard Publishing, 2006), 25.

2. Henry T. Blackaby, *Experiencing God: How to Live the Full Adventure of Knowing and Doing the Will of God* (Nashville, TN: Broadman & Holman, 1994), 24.

Day 15: Apron

1. Rick Warren, *The Purpose Driven Life,* 17.

2. Ken Blanchard, Lead Like Jesus, http://www.leadlikejesus.com/about/default.asp?st=5415 (accessed October 3, 2008).

3. Blanchard, *Lead Like Jesus* (Nashville, TN: W Publishing Group, 2005), 4.

Day 16: Hallways

1. Rusaw and Swanson, *Living a Life on Loan,* 73–74.

2. Diana Pavlac Glyer, *The Company They Keep: C. S. Lewis and J. R. R. Tolkien as Writers in Community* (Kent, OH: Kent State University Press, 2007).

Day 17: Takeout

1. "Reaching Out," Saddleback Church, http://www.saddlebackfamily.com/story/536.html (accessed September 23, 2008).

2. Peg Rose, "Caring for people with HIV/AIDS: What small groups considering this ministry need to know," HIV/AIDS Caring Community, Saddleback Church, http://www.hivandthechurch.com/en-US/StartingAMinistry/Caring_for_people_with_HIVAIDS.htm (accessed October 3, 2008).

3. Pastors.com, http://www.pastors.com/RWMT/?ID=242&artid=9048&expand=1.

4. Rick Warren, P.E.A.C.E., http://www.thepeaceplan.com (accessed September 23, 2008).

Day 18: Does the Body Good

1. Valerie Rae Hanneman, "Serving the Servant," e-Devotional, March 3, 2006, Fresno First e-Ministries, Fresno First Baptist Church, http://www.fresnofirst.org/eministries/archives/000327.html (accessed September 24, 2008).

Day 21: Hourglass

1. MySpace page of Loose Change to Loosen Chains, http://www.myspace.com/lc2lc (accessed September 25, 2008).

Afterword: Day 22: Eye on the Prize

Wikipedia, s.v. "Laminin," http://en.wikipedia.org/wiki/Laminin
September 25, 2008).Explore the Real You with Others